THE TRAVELS AND TRAVAILS OF MUSIC

A TALE OF MUSIC, CULTURE AND RADIO IN THE SOUTH SEAS

Ruth Finnegan

THE TRAVELS AND TRAVAILS OF MUSIC

Bletchley
Callender Press

ISBN 978-1-329-80647-4

www.callenderpress.co.uk

.CONTENTS

PART 4   MUSIC AND MUSICS

Preface

My expectations on reaching Fiji in 1975 for a three-year stay at the University of the South Pacific in the capital, Suva, were rather like those of Beresford Clark's, as described in the first chapter of this book. It is true that as an anthropologist I was willing, at least in principle, to judge people on their own terms, and concede (and it *was* a concession) that European culture might not be the only, or even the best, to exist on this earth.

All the same, steeped as I was in classical literature and Oxford values, I was still essentially the typical ethnocentric ignorant foreigner. Despite my background I still saw Britain, with its professionally trained musicians playing (European) classical works, as the origin and standard of both proper music-making and culture (European high culture naturally).

What I would find in Fiji, I secretly assumed (I think), would, at best, be a reflection of the British-inspired music-making that had travelled, perhaps with difficulty, to this small colonial outpost. There would be nothing - certainly nothing Fiji-originated - to study.

Admittedly I was not alone in such preconceptions. But how wrong we all were (how could I, a field-experienced anthropologist, have been so ethnocentric, so patronising?). And how was different the actual situation - not just then but for many years on, and back.

So the subject of this book is how, arising from and supplementing the insights of Beresford Clark and other earlier visitors (at least unlike countless others they thought the place worth a visit) we can reach a clearer understanding of the movements of musics and cultures in Fiji and, through that, of the world..

This specific account began in 1978 when I was astonished by the numbers and creativity of local musicians. It then, apart from a couple of hastily written and locally published short papers (Finnegan 1978, 1981), for many years lay forgotten, even the typescript lost, while I worked on other things. But then a colleague's chance remark woke me up; it was based on the assumption that culture and radio overseas were necessarily dependent in, even controlled from, London's BBC broadcasts. There was a need for a more balanced - indeed a contrary - understanding

I already knew from my 1978 initial investigation while I was in Fiji, minimal as it was, that that colleague's (widely-shared) perception was far from the mark. But to convince others I needed to go further. 1978 was only one year. Was it special, unusual? What about others in the long history of Fijian and South Seas musicians?

This led me first to the wonderfully detailed BBC Written Archives, then, encouraged by colleagues and with the generous support of a BBC-Overseas grant, to a further research visit to the 2009 Fiji. This, supplemented by further reading, resulted in the present volume.

The book, then, takes three 'moments' to explore something of the complexities of music and its international setting in the island nation of Fiji. These were manifested in people's *action,* in their *uses* of musical forms. So rather than envisaging 'music' itself as 'migrating' or 'travelling ', far less as moving only under the popular (and misleading) title of 'world music', the book stresses instead the musical practices of individuals and groups in a context of changing media (radio one recurrent link), political conflicts and multilateral transnational connections.

Reaching something of this understanding also lay the foundations for my better-known book *The Hidden Musicians* (1989) which I started working on directly after my return to Britain in August 1978. It was from Fiji that I learned to look for, and value, concurrent, and often fluid and blending, musical traditions; the *practices* rather than or, at any rate additional to, text

9

(something I had started to learn in Africa); the importance of the mundane as well as the (so to speak) ethereal dimensions of music; and the art and virtuosity of the apparently 'untrained'.

Without my experience in Fiji *The Hidden Musicians* would never have happened. Both for that and for my widening understanding, still I hope increasing, I owe the musicians and audiences of Fiji an unrepayable debt.

Though it could be further extended I have decided that this account has lain fallow long enough and that it is high time that, despite its deficiencies, it sees the light of day.

RF
Old Bletchley January 2016

Acknowledgements

I am particularly grateful for the opportunity to revisit Fiji for further research in April 2009 which was generously financed by the AHRB 'Tuning in' project arranged for me, with their ever-warm support and encouragement, by my dear Open University colleagues Marie Gillespie and Jason Toynbee.

I am also most grateful to Jason Toynbee (again - who could have a more generous or inspiring colleague) and Byron Dueck for their invitation to the magnificent international 'Migrating Music' conference and for accepting a short preliminary account of the findings there in their *Migrating Music* (2012). Thanks too to the conference participants whose reception encouraged me to think that I did indeed have something worth saying; and, more important, that *Fiji* had something to say, beyond the sometimes somewhat closed sphere of South Pacific specialists, about both music and the linked processes of political, media- and musical change.

For both periods I am indebted to the kindness of many people who gave so generously of their time and knowledge both at the time and some cases in follow-up contact subsequently. Though too numerous to mention individually, I cannot refrain from special thanks, for 1978, to Mrs.

11

Miles of the Fiji Arts Council, all those who so helped me at Fiji's local radio station (FBC), especially Devakar Prasdad, Aminiasi, Gaunavou, that great conductor and human being Saimoni Vatu, Chris Suamawai, Mrs Olga Parshotam, and members of the bands I describe; for 2009, John Wilson, Robin Palmer, Fernando Lobendhal, and Susanna Trnka, and also, very specially, Riyaz Sayed-Khaiyum and the many other unfailingly helpful staff of the Fiji Broadcasting Corporation Limited above Miri of the amazing FBLC Music Library who so wonderfully coordinated my visit.

For documentary sources I thank the wonderful BBC Written Archives Centre in Reading (BBC WAC), specially Jeff Walden, my mentor there, and their permission to reproduce extracts from their holdings; the unparalleled Pacific Collection in the University of the South Pacific Library in Suva and the University of Auckland Library; and the magnificent interlibrary loan service provided by the ever-helpful Open University Library. In addition I have benefited from electronic documentation on the many websites of today, not least those for individual musicians, bands, and other musical organisations, and both learned from and loved (still love) the live streaming of Fijian radio stations.

Introduction

The book takes what might be regarded as a'mini' case study to explore through first-hand research the processes by which at one far-flung spot on the globe music had somehow moved. It sets out to do so not by a sustained chronological narrative of the detail (though that could have been one strategy) but by focusing on the broad situation - musical, political, technological - at three particular 'moments': 1937, 1978 and 2009. These proved good jumping off points for exploring something of the complexities of the changing music(s) and musical activities within the island nation of Fiji in the South Pacific.

Despite its small size, Fiji's musical experience illustrates the limitations of the west-centred paradigms that invoke such concepts as 'modernisation', binary polarities, or epochal periodisation. In Fiji, the contrasting yet interlaced activities and aspirations of three major musical traditions - Pacific, European and Indian - date back several centuries in a region criss-crossed by long international links but rather seldom encompassed within popular music studies. Their musical traditions were and are manifested in the *actions* of people as they both stayed and moved in old and new diasporas, and in associated ideologies of 'authenticity' alongside innovation.

The book thus takes one particular case study to investigate the processes by which at one far-flung spot on the globe musical practices had somehow moved or at any rate changed . But rather than, as more often, envisaging 'music' itself as 'migrating' or 'travelling', far less as only existent under the misleading label of 'world music', the book focuses instead on the musical actions of individuals and groups in a context of changing media (with radio as one recurrent link), political divisions and multilateral transnational connections.

PART 1 THE FIJI OF 1937

Chapter 1 A visit to the island of Fiji

In the early morning of a Thursday - July 29[th,] 1937, the year of the Coronation of George VI of England - a young man disembarked from the SS *Mariposa:* 'a most comfortable and artistic ship', he writes, in the language of the day, but alas 'poor service in the dining saloon'[1].

He alighted in Suva, capital of the British colony of Fiji in the South Pacific, complete with his two trunks, expanding suitcase, array of evening dress and diner jackets, toupee and hat box. [2] He was personally met by the Colonial Governor's Adjutant and taken to stay at Government House. And there he was fittingly entertained and monitored.

The young man was Mr J. B. Clark, Director of the BBC's new and ambitious Empire Service. He was spending 6 days in Fiji as part of the grand Empire Tour which for 6 months in 1937 took him round the world, travelling by the then

---

[1] E4/22 Empire Service, J. B. Clark's Tour X (Diary Notes) 1936-38, BBC WAC. .

[2] BBC Memo DES to DP 15 March 1937, E4/13 Empire Service JB Clark's tour I 1936-1937,

17

slow (by modern standards) transport available from Malta to Ceylon, Australia, Fiji, New Zealand, Hong Kong, Malaya, and India (his planned Middle East and Gibraltar sections had to be cancelled at the last minute). Its aims, approved by the Colonial Office as well as the BBC, were 'to establish contacts, discuss mutual problems with broadcasters overseas, and study reactions to the Empire Service'[3].

It was a timely project, planned with careful circumspection to follow up and extend the 1936 Colonial Office report on 'how to accelerate the provision of broadcasting services in the Colonial Office' in coordination with the BBC ('Plymouth Report' 1936: 1). It was also, less visibly, an undercover attempt by the BBC and the Government to counter German propaganda and strengthen Britain's dominance of the communications lines by more effective Imperial broadcasts[4].

So now Beresford Clark had reached Suva, the capital of the Fijian Islands. From one point of view these were just a few small specks in the

---

[3] letter JCWR to Shelley 20 Feb. 1937, E4/13, BBC WAC
[4] Cutting from *Sydney Morning Herald* 26/2/37, and Letter from A.M.Crofton Nova Scotia 29 March 1937, both in Empire Service, JB Clark's tour I 1936-7, E4/13, BBC WAC.

South Pacific Ocean (even now, as we found when we were planning our stay there, they are quite hard to find, and re-find too, on a map of the world, even on a map of just the Pacific Ocean). From another perspective however they were by far the largest and most important of the many island colonies in that great ocean, long established as a crucial node on international liner routes both within the Pacific and between Australia and America.

Among the Pacific islands the main island of Fiji, Vanua Levu, was the only one so far to have its own broadcast radio system. It had its own international importance too for it formed an essential link on the unbroken chain of the stations that operated the (important) Pacific Cable from Vancouver Island to Australia and New Zealand (*Handbook of Fiji* 1962: 196).

So what did Clark find in Fiji? In his notes on his visit [5] he recounts staying at the Governor's residence, being shown around by the aide-de-camp, his invitations to tea and tennis, being entertained to dinner at a series of houses, and the company he enjoyed there; these were the conventional occupations of a visitor within what was by now something of an English-speaking diaspora in this small island.

---

[5] Notes on visit to Fiji, E4/22 BBC WAC

There was also an evening at Government House listening to gramophone records of -predictably really - one of Gilbert and Sullivan's operas, in this case *Ruddigore* ('one of the best recollections of my tour' he was to say later[6]). He also spent many hours with the manager of the local radio station – of which more in a moment – with whom he forged what became a lifelong link, met the great and good among the local European community of whom there were around 5000 in Fiji at the time, attended and spoke - no doubt forcefully with the full might if the Empire and the BBC behind him - the first meeting of the Fiji Broadcasting Committee, specially set up for his visit. He broadcast a short talk from the newly built local studio, and sampled the BBC's offerings while trying to resolve persistent complaints from its English listeners (again, more on this shortly).

Despite the dress clothes and the social round it was an intensive visit of setting up contacts and exploring the local broadcasting situation. It was productive too in laying foundations for further local developments and interactions at the international level, and was followed up in later years by a remarkable set of continuing

---

[6] letter Clark to Lady Richards 24 Dec. 1937, Empire Service, JB Clark's tour VI 1937-8, E4/18, BBC WAC

correspondence: Clark was adept at forming continuing warm personal links, an essential quality as he rose steadily through the ranks of the BBC. In Fiji as in other places he visited Clark did indeed seem to succeed in his aim of creating a network of acquaintances and correspondents throughout the then British world, putting local practitioners in touch with those elsewhere and using his good offices to share experience. The Empire had its advantages.

And the music he encountered while there? Both from his BBC brief and, no doubt, his own outlook as a child of his time - of England, of the Empire as it then was - his focus was naturally on European music. Live music in the great concert halls of London or Edinburgh or Manchester would have been his ideal setting, but both locally and when away from home and abroad what was then known as 'bottled' music had its place too. Thus gramophone records were the widely circulated current medium – witness Clark's entertainment with a *Ruddigore* evening at the Governor's residence, no doubt one of many such sessions for local residents. Accordingly collections of gramophone record are continually mentioned as valuable possessions for Europeans in the far-flung empire, a medium through which they could continue to hear their precious (home) music.

But it was radio, both direct and rebroadcast, that was the coming medium. It was on this that hopes were laid for the circulation of music at a distance both within European countries and among the diasporic communities overseas. It was a channel which with its sense of immediacy, increasing accessibility, and adaptability over the years was coming to be the key medium for the capturing and transmission of music at a distance and one to which we will need to keep coming back in this brook .

Radio was not a self-evident medium however, nor was Fiji a particularly easy location. I will not go into the complex technological issues, but there had been and still were decisions to be made about the allocation of frequencies or the respective merits of wireless as against wired (i.e. over telephone lines) transmission, and over medium or short wave (both arguably needed in Fiji with its combination of a relatively dense population in parts of the main island with a widely scattered population through its many islands).

There was also the 12-hour time difference between Fiji and Britain to be taken into account, then a real problem in technical terms, the lengthy and complex routes which transmissions had to traverse, both affected, it turned out, by the time of year and by the sunspot cycle:all problems which nowadays we can afford to ignore. Even for the few areas with electricity there was also the problem , even for the relatively few (Europeans of course) who *did* possess radio sets that heavy and bulky batteries that were the only resources then available were if course continually running out and their replacement precarious and unpredictable. You might *possess* a set -but radio silence was maybe equally frequent when ships did not bring a re-charged battery before the spare ran out.

By 1937 the BBC Empire radio service was up to a point heard in Fiji. By then about 700 radio licences had been issued in the colony, overwhelmingly to European and what were then termed 'half-caste' listeners . They could sometimes pick up overseas broadcasts from the BBC but also – for England was *not* the only player in the game – at times from Australia, New Zealand and (most loudly) Germany. There was also the recently established local station, a bone of contention which we shall return to soon. [7] The BBC Empire service transmitted from Daventry with its mix of news, documentaries and music was now coming through reasonably well, a contrast to some years earlier when the

---

[7] Empire service policy qv E4/10 esp 1937 Report incl figures: Fiji Eur pop = 4763, coloured 192,686, no. of wireless licences 730, no. of potential short-wave listeners 1000). 671 licence in all in June 1937, [figures in E4/48]. [also Rome, Hong Kong, America E4/28.list of about 60 short-wave stations operating in 1929 in E4/2].

BBC's broadcasts, however well-intentioned, were essentially inaudible throughout the Pacific.

It attracted a body of loyal listeners however, keen as so many were throughout the empire to be in touch with the mother country, and hear the BBC's broadcasts of great national events, the chimes of Big Ben, and the various genres of western music (however much these were argued over[8]). Throughout the Empire members of the

---

[8] See E4/38 for the polarised criticisms of 'dull highbrow stuff' on the one side and 'hot jazz and crooning' on the other (lovers of 'serious music' specially liked the Empire Orchestra, those on the light side military bands, theatre organ, light orchestral combinations; dance orchestras). Some listeners as well as forces within the BBC were concerned to keep to the 'pure' original tradition, with 'crooning' drawing particular diatribes and 'vocals' for a time consequently suspicious, as to some was jazz, regarded as extraneous and 'negroid' (see R27/71/1, R27/71/2, R34/281, Jazz R27/946/1), expressed for example by an otherwise appreciative listener from Canada

> We have inflicted on us ... some rubbish bearing the high-falutin' title of 'Facets of Syncopation', and this odious jazz programme is to be repeated in Transmission 6 tonight.... If you imagine you are giving us over here something to enthuse about you are sadly mistaken. Such blithering twaddle and raucous row is available to listeners here from scores of 500-watt stations with their tooth-paste, jam-soup-pickle advertising programmes at any time of day (Empire Mailbag,

English-speaking diaspora warmed to this link to home, their views (not always uncritical) coming through in letters to the regular 'Empire Mail Bag' in the BBC's *Empire Programme Pamphlet.* A 'middle-aged exile' (location unspecified) enthuses

> I must thank you for the great pleasure you give us here, far from good old England. When I first used the receiver, your greeting, Big Ben, and then the National Anthem, moved us profoundly – it took quite a time to listen without real emotion. I don't think we realised until then just how much Home meant to us (*Empire Programme Pamphlet* Vol. VIII, Dec. 2. 1936: 2)

Or again (from the Argentine but from the shared tone of these communications it could equally well have been from anywhere, including Fiji)

> So, dear BBC, let us, the middle-aged exiles, wallow in what a young modern friend calls 'a slosh of sentiment', and give us as many of the old favourites as possible (*loc cit*).

Empire Programme Pamphlet III no. 24, 12 May 1937),

A similar attachment to this voice of the empire came from listeners in Fiji, not least in their passionate objections to the interference with BBC broadcasts both by German transmissions and by the newly opened local radio station. The Radio Listeners Association of Fiji (a highly articulate if not necessarily representative body) petitioned the Acting Governor, and a regular listener complained

> The [local] station is an infernal nuisance to seriously-minded listeners as its [*sic*] mostly cheap gramophone music and advertisements cause considerable interference and restricts the reception of overseas programmes (Radio Listeners Association Memorial to Acting Governor 14 Nov 1936, E1/1124/1, BBC WAC).

As the elite, licensed listeners, they felt 'entitled to listen to the Empire Broadcasts - 'daily and special', such as t the Coronation celebrations, and a 'fair hearing on the air' (*loc. cit.*). later letter insisted 'I trust that ... on your return to the Old Country you will not forget to let the B.B.C. know how eager we English are to get their voice in this part of the world'. [9] These after all were

---

[9] letter R C Farquhar to Malcolm Frost June 1938, E1/1124/2, BBC WAC.

the people to whom the BBC saw itself speaking - the 'white populations under the British flag' - with the Empire Service directed to 'those sections of the colonial populations to which its contents are suitable'[10]. To the English-speaking diaspora in Fiji the BBC was a line to their own cultural heritage.

The programmes they listened to were a mixture of news, documentaries, dramas and, notably, music, classical, light classical and popular: orchestras, soloists, military bands, dance bands, theatre organs. During Clark's stay he could have heard, for example, a Chopin recital, several brass bands, the BBC Singers, BBC Orchestra, dance music by 'Carroll Gibbons and the Savoy Hotel Orphans', Victor Sylvester and his Ballroom Orchestra, Old Tyme Music Hall, the 'Airs of Ulster' by the BBC Northern Ireland Orchestra, religious services (with hymns) on the Sunday, and a selection of instrumental and vocal recitals, both solo and small group (the programmes are listed in the *Empire Programme Pamphlet* 1937).

---

[10] Report on Empire Broadcasting November 1929, Empire Service Policy 1928-9, E4/2, BBC WAC (also 'in proportion as native populations develop an interest in broadcasting, the local service will provide the natives with programmes of their own type'; Plymouth report' 1936: 1-2

Not that he had much time for actual listening. But he did tune in - or try to - a couple of times and had to agree with the complaints he had heard from some of BBC's 'faithful and regular listeners' about local electrical devices. He could hear 'London log' (a talk) fairly clearly and some of Orchestre Raymonde, but in his notes on the occasion was in 'no doubt that something should be done about the interference from refrigerators, dirty fan-brushes and a washing machine ... not really entertainment value'. Listening to the BBC was not straightforward, and music above all was the sufferer [11].

The new station about which BBC listeners were so indignant was in fact a crucial step in Fiji's radio history, the very one that was to become the basis of all its later flourishing local stations. It began in a small way. First had been a contract to Amalgamated Wireless (Australasia) Ltd (AWA) to run the exiting wireless-telegraph service in Suva (as so often, history progresses in small increments of the familiar rather than great revolutionary leaps into the unknown). This was then extended into a license from the Fiji Posts and Telegraphs Department, typical child of

---

[11] reception problems continued even after his visit cf letter R C Farquhar to Malcolm Frost June 1938, E1/1124/2, BBC WAC.

empire, to start up local radio in 1935 with the call sign ZJV.

The agreement was that this new station would 'carry out a regular service daily' except - characteristic of the time - on Sundays. This was to last in total each week 'for a period of at least four hours, consisting of a programme of music, entertainment, instruction, public announcements and other matter, which shall be approved by the Postmaster-General' . Advertising would be permitted for not more than 10% of the time [12].

The service had got going in 1935. It was operated from two small rooms in Suva. One one held the medium wave transmitter and racks of gramophone records, the other a studio where an announcer sat at the control desk in the one. It was run by the then powerful Amalgamated Wireless (Australasia) Ltd (AWA) through its local subsidiary Fiji Broadcasting Co. Ltd.

This local service was for Fiji's 'Europeans'. The 'entertainments' Clark and others with receivers could have heard were mainly in the form of

---

[12] Department of Posts and Telegraphs Broadcasting Licence 1935, in Fiji Broadcasting Service File 1 1932-1937, E/1/1124/1, BBC WAC and Committee on Broadcasting Services in the Colonies Sub-Committee Paper 55, Memorandum on broadcasting in Fiji, E4/31, BBC WAC.

musical recordings: varied items but, as AWA put it, 'with a tendency to restrict jazz artists, syncopaters and crooners' [13]. Most broadcasts probably came from gramophone records but there were also retransmissions of important overseas broadcasts like the king's speeches. From January 1937 it had started to include one hour in Fijian between 8 and 9 p.m. once a week: news, talks, and entertainment such as Fijian folk songs, native singing and music [14].

Initially there were relatively few receiving sets, predominantly owned by residents of European origin. Of approximately 1000 radio licences in 1938 only 30 were held by 'natives'. Interest - and patronage - grew quite rapidly however and by the end of that year about 7000 Fijians were said to listen regularly to about 145 sets, listening, as was common in the tropical empire at that time, on a communal out-if-doors basis. [15] E4/31, E1/1124/2.

---

[13] Publicity O.S. Amalgamated Wireless (Australasia) Ltd, 25 Oct. 1935 E12/8 BBC WAC. The quotation is taken from publicity for the opening of a similar AWA service in Papua New Guinea in 1935 but there is no reason to believe the fare was different in Fiji.
[14] E4/28. BBC WAC [?]

Nothing was at that point directed to the other main element of the native population – the Indians (of whom more in Chapter 3)"on the rather specious grounds that'There is no evidence as yet that the Indian will react to broadcasting as rapidly as the Fijian has done' [sic] [16](Report of committee [on] broadcasting, Fiji Broadcasting Service File 2a, 1938-, E1/1124/2 BBC WAC), or, as the local organiser put it, he knew little of what Indians wanted to listen to as either talks or musical entertainment:

> For obvious reasons, [sic] we have been reluctant to hand over the microphone to Indians who have occasionally approached us; and we have no knowledge whatever of Indian music. Presumably, recordings of this are obtainable ... [More work needs to be done on this by those] well versed in Indian affairs (F. C. Exon, Memorandum to Broadcasting Cttee, E1/1124/2).

During his visit Clark spent many hours with the manager of the local radio station (one of his briefs was to courage local broadcasting), Frank Exon. The two men struck up a warm

---

[16] Report of committee [on] broadcasting, Fiji Broadcasting Service File 2a, 1938-, E1/1124/2 BBC WAC.

relationship of mutual respect that was to continue for nearly 20 years.

A broadcasting committee was also set up, its first meeting taking place during Clark's stay, eventuating fairly rapidly in proposals both to continue with re-broadcasting BBC material and, crucially, to extend the current offerings into more substantial provision for natives (4 hours each for Fijian and Indian listeners per week), proposals which, in the style of the 1930s were duly discussed by the BBC and the Colonial Office in London and negotiated with the local company. There were concerns about the advertising, seen as a deplorable but in the end necessary concomitant, and as it was noted in the London discussion 'Mr Clark thought that the saving factor ... was that Mr Exon ... was genuinely keen on broadcasting' [17].

In terms of music, then, Clark did indeed encounter European music of various kinds during his stay in Fiji. It reached him and others in this imperial setting through the media of gramophone records and (if with problems) through radio transmissions accessible to the local English-speaking diaspora in Fiji.

---

[17] Committee on Broadcasting Services in the Colonies Sub-Committee Paper 57 Notes on meeting of 19 Dec 1938, E4/31, BBC WAC

But what did Mr Clark *not* find? or at any rate not see or report? In terms of music - a great deal. For that small colony of Fiji was in fact already home to complex musical traditions and the locale for more diasporas than one.

For we need to understand a much more complex picture than suggested in the narrative, common enough in 1937 and to an extent still continuing, of Fiji as a primitive, isolated and native community standing in contrast to the civilisations of the west. Some saw, amped still see, this tradition, how misleading in practice, as something precious, to be preserved at all costs, or, at the very lesst least not hastened into contexts like the market economy or urban culture.

Thus was the viewpoint that underlay the first Governor's approach, one which was to have such a crucial influence on all of Fiji's later history. Others started from the same premise, but saw the future otherwise: of a community destined in time, with careful nurturing, to take on modern media – above all literacy and in due course recorded material and telecommunications - so as to 'catch up' with the cultural and internationally vibrant sophistication of the developed world: that is, of the west, the accepted standard of evaluation. Either way, the native Fijian state was conceptualised as essentially the uncontaminated initial base on which history could now start working.

Certainly Clark had aspirations for the local development, eventually, of 'special programmes for natives' and in Fiji as elsewhere in the empire was set to encourage this. It was a project, limited as it might seem by modern evaluation, of genuine sincerity and, within the concepts of its time, democratisation. But for the moment the BBC's offerings were directed towards the *British* diaspora whether in Fiji or elsewhere in the English-speaking colonies. Clark was a notable pioneer and leader but he was also was after all, and understandably (what else could he have been?) a child of his time and had some excuse for taking London as the centre, just as today – with less excuse - Euro-America is still so often assumed as the paradigm and centre of gravity.

But, given all that – were there things he did *not* see - and, child of his age, *could* not see?

Chapter 2 What Mr Clark did not hear: the music of the South Pacific

Unseen and totally unappreciated by Clark (by almost all other Europeans too) was one essential fact: that Fiji was already the site of three major and complex musical traditions.

He was correct of course in his assumption that European music – to simplify a complex series of variants under that label –was indeed an important force in the local arena, emanating primarily from Britain and captured on gramophone records and broadcasts from the northern hemisphere's BBC in London. It is true that in practice these reached the local European diaspora as much from Australia and New Zealand as direct from London. Fiji after all was an international communications node, with a long history of contacts across the Pacific and beyond and already operating in something of a regional and Pacific setting, not just an imperial one. But London was the source and the authirity to which the European population in Fiji looked. It remained their imaginative home for culture as for affection and loyalty.

But –what about the locally generated musical activity in Suva at the time? This was something that, given his mission, Clark would naturally not have been concerned with. No doubt he would have shared the opinion of an earlier BBC visitor to Fiji that 'you will appreciate, of course, that there is no local talent at all available' [18]. But we can be sure that, in true colonial-diaspora fashion, there were hymns in the many Christian churches that had been built in Suva for the Europeans working there (the Anglican church at least would surely have had a choir and organ), that one or more brass bands played, that English songs were sung in the schools, and that the widespread enthusiasm for Gilbert and Sullivan throughout the empire of the time would have been evident not only in gramophone records (those short always-to-be -changed 78rpm discs on wind-up Masters Voice boxes) but also in active sung and instrumental performances.

Even less audible not only to transient visitors but also to the vast majority of the local European population of Fiji (there were a few notable exceptions) was the rich and long-established musical heritage of the Pacific islands. At one level these outdoor and in one way ubiquitous performances should have been and perhaps were unmissable. But as with humans everywhere, because they were unfamiliar they were simply not heard. Or, as in other contexts with jazz and, later, rock they were

---

[18] letter from Malcom Frost, 18 May 1933, E4/46, BBC WAC

noticed merely as 'noise', 'din', even as offensive. Not as *music*.

Further, the Fiji Islands – the disparate group making up the colony of Fiji (an archipelago rather than as commonly pictured a single island) - did not belong to one monolithic culture, as often assumed, but included diverse dialects and political allegiances. As with other islands of the South Pacific they were both separated and linked by vast tracts of ocean. In Fiji's case they were closely connected to and influenced by many neighbouring islands (neighbouring in Pacific terms that is).

In Fiji's case it was particular bonds with the island of Tonga . It was from there that the highest chiefs in one powerful area of Fiji had come, with relationships of kinship and allegiance constantly cultivated, and in whose cultural heritage, not least their famous musical traditions (described in 19xx) , many Fijian islands actively and continually participated. Elsewhere these were replaced or supplemented by other Pacific genres, adding to the musical diversity of the archipelago.

Both colonial governors and missionaries to Fiji had, in their own interests, long been trying by various means to weld these heterogeneous elements together, not altogether successfully. The scene remained diverse and constantl changing. Contrary to the model assumed by European visitors and residents - and still, less forgiveably, sometimes assumed (or wished) in west-centred analyses - there was no one fixed or homogenous 'tradition'.

Amidst these diversities however certain musical genres from the complex worlds of Pacific music *were* widely recognised. Let me stress that they were *many*, and diverse. This was a complex and sophisticated musical tradition, and, like anywhere else, local and regional fashions changed over time. The favourite genres were primarily vocal though also sometimes with some (limited)'instrumental input. Amidst the almost infinite number of (changing and changeable) forms, such as lullabies (*sere ni vakamoce gone*), and songs for canoeing (*vakalutuivoce* – literally 'dipping of the oars', sung while paddling), war (*cibi*), and fishing, let me pick out three for special mention.

First, indisputably, was the *meke*. This was the group dance-song genre held in the highest esteem. It had strong chiefly and ceremonial connections, and a long and dignified history behind it, for Fijian music too had its high culture and one with powerful elite connections. It was long-lasting, as elite music so often is. The *meke* (there is no simple English translation, and the Fijian word, fittingly, has become the accepted term) has over many generations changed little in its essentials. It was noted as an elaborate and frequently practised form by 19th-century observers (e.g. Williams 1870: 113-9). Missionaries often (though not invariably) took a poor view of its pagan connections but were also in some cases impressed by how readily local converts used the respected and effective *meke* form to convey a Christian message in Fijian words (Williams 1870: 117, 119).

In its somewhat elastic senses (is not music always so?) the *meke* has lasted well into recent times, up to the present. It was already adaptable to current situations in the mid-19th century. A firsthand observer in 1929, shortly before Clark's visit, commented on how 'Fijians still love their *mekes*'. One of the few prepared to notice, he described a 50 minute performance by 70 men and women celebrating 'the death of a chieftain of the olden time', with singing for about half the time together with beautiful co-ordinated dances, praised for its 'grace, regularity of movement, sense of time and rhythm' – and above all 'joyousness' (Henderson 1931: 70-71, 89). Another example was the ceremonious and impressive *meke* enactment before a Fijian high chief that had been composed to honour and commemorate the two Fijian representatives who had attended George VI's Coronation in May 1937.

The movement of the dancers were interpretations of the departure of the two men in a big boat with two 'chimneys'; their arrival at Westminster Abbey; and the placing of crowns on the heads of the king and queen. The men and women taking part in the dance were dressed in native tapa or bark cloth, their limbs glistening with coconut oil. The chant of the story was accompanied by the rhythmic beating of a *lali*, or native wooden drum (Coulter 1942: 33).

As with other high-culture forms there were a number of sub-genres within the *meke*, with differing degrees of popularity. But in its iconic classic form it was strongly associated with chiefship and public ritual. Essentially it was a group-performance, made up of voices harmonising and intertwining in sophisticated three-fold layering. The dancers, either standing or (in the beautiful Pacific style) sitting, brought out the meaning of the words in their amazingly tightly coordinated movements. Strongly rhythmic, the singing was accompanied by a wooden *lali* gong, clapping, and bamboo tubes striking out the beat on the ground. The performance was visual as well as acoustic for as well as the choreography the costumes, shell ornaments, leaves, flowers,fragrances and oiled bodies of the performers were also prominent features of the display. Some *mekes* were remembered for many years, a way, as some Fijians put it, of 'recording our history'.

They were also characterised by their special, inspired, mode of composition. This process, in some respects unusual but in others not really so unfamiliar, deserves some description and explanation. The expert composer, known as the *daunivucu*, entered a state of trance or dream, then, inspired from the spirit world, uttered aloud the musical and poetic text.

This was captured by his companions on the spot, an essential stage, for on waking from his trance or sleep - a kind of self-hypnotised or possession state - the poet-composer often could not remember the words which the spirits had inspired him with. The assistants therefore 'recorded' the words either using the remarkable Pacific memorising powers (on which see ...) or, more recently, on portable tape recorders. Sometimes the process, or so I was told, took place on that dangerous liminal spot between coral reef and deep ocean where the poet (traditionally male) deliberately stationed himself; at other times it was by the side of the sea or in a village after the composer had stupefied himself by leaves designed to have precisely this effect.

The composition stage was followed by lengthy rehearsals by massed choir of singers and dancers to perfect -and amazingly so - the combined expression of words, music, and gestures before the final grand performance. By then, with its multi-media arts.the result was more a ballet - to use an English term - than just a 'song'. It was usually held before a chief or other important figure and it was he and not the composer, rehearsal leader or performers who, in Fijian ideology, held the right and the responsibility for authorising future performances.

This account gives a somewhat simplified description of what happened, one that would however probably be accepted by most Fijians [19]. As so often with anything musical, there were many variations, known particularly to those with special expertise in this high art. There were grades if composers, the highest – this was unusual - being those with the capacity to be inspired with the dance gestures as well as words and music –a rare endowment. In recent times certain university students – I have known them – and choir-masters in the ubiquitous Methodist churches still compose *makes,* often now in a fully-fledged immediate written rather than, as in the past, oral form, in a kind of trance which, for

---

19 For further accounts of the *meke* see Glamuzina 2001, Kaisau 1978, Kubuabola et al. 1978, Lee 1998, Tuqota 2006: esp 39ff and references there.

them, is a clear version of the established *meek* tradition.

For most Fijians Christian religious music took an equally important, if different, role, in practice more regularly performed than the grand *meke* events. It was everywhere and took various forms, but above all it was the singing of hymns. By the 1930s Christianity was no incoming religion but a deeply embedded and pervasive dimension of local Fijian culture. Predominantly Methodist but also including many other denominations, the local churches may have originally been missionary-led but by the 1930s, and in fact long before, were now thoroughly the possession of indigenous Fijians.

Christianity had in fact reached Fiji not direct from Europe, as we might assume, but by missionaries from the neighbouring and overwhelmingly Christian island of Tonga. This island was also the origin- and high-status point of reference for the deeply Christian chiefly families in several parts of Fiji where to an extent chiefs and church went together.

Shortly before Clark's visit, there had been the grand 1935 cclebrations to mark the centenary of Fiji Methodist Mission, with ceremonial gifts to Tongan representatives to salute their contribution, and participation from relatives of the early native Tongan missionaries who 'brought the gospel' to Fiji. This was merely one example of the continuing link and sense of obligation, even allegiance, by the Fijians to Tinga and its traditional chiefs and royal family (an island well known even in Britain from the prominent part played by Tinga's Queen Salote at King George V's Coronation where, tall and imposing, she was the only dignitary to sit in an uncovered open carriage in the pouring rain).

Hymns had taken on huge importance, sung both by full congregations and by specially rehearsed choirs in the Fijian mode. The words were in Fijian, sometimes translated from the English and to tunes similar to or reminiscent of European counterparts, but also with locally-influenced melodies, their style influenced by older Fijian forms. This style was even more marked in the *same*, the sung 'psalms', and the other responses in weekly worship: these often entirely followed the *meke* musical texture in their style.

In the hymns, singers were readily able to adapt the layered voices of traditional *meke* song– or so it has been argued – to the European four-part-harmony tradition. All the same they were unmistakably sung in the resonant unaccompanied Fijian-voiced style which made the end result both familiar and different to European ears. Often, as with *meke* singing, the singers had memorised the words and tunes but also in time came the convenient medium solfa-notation which was added the hymnbooks which many church member now possessed.

Indeed – a surprise to many outsiders - hymnbooks in Fijian had been published by local printing presses for nearly a century (Henderson 1931: 190-91). As an English visitor in 1937/8 described it 'with a native hymn book every word of the singing could easily be followed ... the men's voices were especially musical, more so than the women's. I don't think I have heard a richer tone anywhere' ('Tourist' 1937: 141). Hymns were thus hugely influential, and of daily not just weekly occurrence.

But we must also note the popularity of certain European – well, by then world-wide – works, Above all it was Handel's *Messiah*, a continuing favourite in so many Pacific islands, sung, often unaccompanied, in local style. The 1935 centenary celebrations included an unaccompanied Fijian choir singing the 'Hallelujah chorus'(Burton and Deane 1936:127), a tradition long to continue. By the 1930s in other words any account of Fijian music as practised by Fijians would inevitably have to include the performance of hymns and oratorios by the many Methodist Church singers.

As in so many other places in the world, the English brass band tradition had also reached Fiji, the third form that by now was a significant presence in the Fijian musical scene. An 'English visitor' saw a boat being 'played off' by a Fijian brass band in 1937, its members all reading from printed scores ('Tourist' 1937: 141), and the military forces, which from the 1st world war had included Fijians, would certainly have had their own band (it definitely had by 1939) playing marches and other music from the extensive British brass band repertoire – another tradition that has continued to this day.

Such examples remind us again that Fiji as elsewhere had already by 1937 – indeed long before - seen many historical changes and international connections. Its music was by no means made up of impervious tradition (another popular outsider's stereotype,for Pacific islands, alas, as for Africa). Rather it consisted of a selective exploitation of a range of available styles and repertoires. This came through too in the popular forms being sung in the 1930s Fiji, the outcome of already lengthy interaction between local musical styles and European and American popular music.

At first this 'popular music' (not, as has often been pointed out, a very satisfactory term but used here for want of anything better) mostly just meant setting Fijian words to existing European tunes. But soon musicians were composing both words and melody, drawing not only on western musical styles but also on models from elsewhere in the Pacific and the Caribbean. The lively *taralala* songs, dating back to before 1900, apparently arose from contacts with western popular music (the name possibly deriving from the English *tra-la-la*), songs for mixed-sex couple dancing and highly popular with the youth (Lee 1998: 780). Another example were the *sere ni cumu*, literally 'bumping songs' which started as bar songs in the 1920s when Fijians were for the first time legally allowed to buy beer and drink it in public. They then, in typically Fijian style, became popular during the informal drinking sessions that so often, then and later, formed the setting for sociability informal singing (Goldsworthy 1998: 161).

The musical complexity and historical changes evident in Fiji dent the common image of primordial Pacific islanders and age-old close-to-nature tradition. That wishful romantic image still persists, however, the more so in this age that so often privileges 'green' 'back-to-nature' ideologies and ethnic nationalism. It evokes palm trees, the 'Pacific way', and indigenous natives struggling with the European colonial and, in due course, postcolonial worlds to retain their own deep-rooted culture. But this image was already outdated in the Fiji of 1937 – if for no other reason that by then nearly half the population were of Indian extraction.[20]

---

[20] 1936 Census: European 4,028, Part-European 4,574, Fijian 97,651, Fiji Indian 85,002, 'Others' ?, total 198,379 (Mayer 1973: 7).

Chapter 3 The ones that Mr Clark did not hear: Fiji's Indians

Indians? in Fiji?

Yes indeed. They were there as part of the massive influx – import really – of indentured labourers that brought huge number of Indians to work on the local sugar plantations, work for which the colonial government of the time, close patron and friend of the local chiefs, thought indigenous Fijians unsuited (or, some would say, too 'lazy). 'Europeans' of course were not in question for such work.

So - between 1879 and 1916, over 60,000 indentured labourers arrived in 'coolie ships' from India. This was a deliberate policy, initiated in the late 19th century by the first colonial Governor Sir Arthur Gordon, with consequences for life in Fiji – and its music – right up to the present. His aim was to preserve the native Fijians' 'traditional lifestyle' undisrupted by the industrial and commercial economy. The then Australian-owned sugar plantations needed labourers, and Indians – unlike Pacific Islanders – were deemed suitable for the work.

This policy meant –and was designed to mean - that the so-called' native Fijians', whose interests were to be paramount, would be sheltered from commerce, retaining their land (of which nearly 90 percent was held in inalienable right by native Fijians). They could thus continue undisturbed in their villages under their traditional chiefs.

These incomers did not at first see themselves as 'Indian', They were individuals from differing locations, religions, castes and languages, with no common ties except for enduring common conditions of work and perhaps having been on the same ship together. But, lumped together as they were under the common name of 'cooolies' and juxtaposed to 'native Fijians', the idea of their 'Indian-ness' began form, in time taking overt political forms, assisted further by the emerging shared language of the Fijian version of Hindi. The consciousness of being 'Indians in Fiji' was further reinforced by the colonial government's policy of residential segregation and emphasis on a contrast between Indians and Fijians – yet another strategy for welding together disparate Fijian sections into some kind of a whole.

At first living in the harsh conditions of 'the lines' – not, many would say, so unlike slave concentrations - many Indians opted at the end of their contracts not to return home but to settle in Fiji: at least, unlike slaves, they had those option be.,Other immigrants (Gujarati traders,

Punjabi agriculturalists) arrived from India of their own choice something which could not be aid of all the earlier labourers, These had, apparently, often been misled in India about where and how they were going and about the constraints on their movement, employment or wages to which they would be subjected. This later influx came mainly in the 1920s after the abolition of the indenture system in 1920.

By 1937 thereforeq there was already a large Indian population, and as a result Indians and their music were well established in Fiji. They were by then mostly working as tenant farmers in sugar plantations and, unlike Fijians, active in commerce and industry. A local study based on field research from 1937 gives a colourful – and convincing - picture of their variety

> Fiji's Indian population of 100,000, made up of various sects and creeds, is always a surprise to visitors: turbaned Moslems and Hindus; tall, bearded Sikhs; and Madrassis with their gaily attired womenfolk; Bombay tailors busily plying their trade; farmers, shoemakers, laundrymen, taxidrivers, clerks, and household servants – all represent the numerous occupations to which the Indian in Fiji has readily turned his hand. As one contemplates a street scene, a Hindu sadhu (ascetic) passes along in

yellow robes with occult sect marks painted on his brow in white and vermilion. A haughty Mohammedan fakir with an inflated goatskin slung over his shoulder tries – with a proud attempt at unconcern – to get out of the way of an automobile (Coulter 1942: 1).

The 'Indians' had thus by the 1930s become an accepted portion of the tripartite Fijian polity – Europeans, Fijians, Indians. Though with different rights and status from the native Fijians, by the time of Clark's visit in 1937 the immigrant Indians had become 'almost as indigenous as the Fijians themselves', as a contemporary observer put it (in Burton and Deane 1936: 106). More than half of them were by then Fiji-born and – a continuing and growing anxiety to the native Fijian- and European-dominated government - soon near to outnumbering the native Fijians: indeed - a continuing surprise to outsiders - for much of the 20th century they would actually be in the majority.

At the same time the economic and political conditions meant that they lived somewhat separate lives from the land-owning and chief-ruled native Fijians. They were interested and inspired by their common membership of the British Empire, a large factor in many of their lives, not least those who had gone through the British educational system as it transferred to Fiji (grammar-school inclined of course). The Indians at the same time also, unlike the native Fijian or European populations, looked less to Britain than to India, the motherland. It was the ties to *India* that they cherished, both symbolically and practically, whether in politics, education, religion, personal communication ,or – the relevant point here – musical, fashions.

This then was the background for the strong Indian musical tradition within Fiji. Not that this was a simple matter. The migrants, remember, came from many different backgrounds as to place, language, caste and, an important dimension, religion: the majority were Hindu and from North India, but there were also later waves from the south making for a sizeable Muslim minority.

This diversity makes simplified generalisation about their music unwise, not least because of the frequent interactions with the changing genres and influences of South Asia and India. But it can be said that from the start the Indian 'coolies' worked at perpetuating forms of their religious song and recitations. It is striking how soon and how extensively musical activity resumed, indeed continued, even in the early indenture years of near slave-like conditions in 'the lines'.

It was the religious context that provided the impetus and framework. From the start indentured labourers in Fiji – about three-quarters Hindu – met regularly to sing together and to recite from that great religious text, the *Ramayana*. Or rather, amidst the conflicting traditions and options, they eventually settled on the Tulsidas version of the *Ramayana* and the Hindu *bhakti* devotional tradition with its focus on singing and prayer.

This in time became profoundly influential in Fiji. Even during the strictly-controlled early indenture period, groups met weekly in the evenings or weekends to engage in the religious duty of musical recitals of the text – the valued mode. Dramatic re-enactments of the Ram story in the annual *Ramlila* festival were already being staged early in the twentieth century, usually lasting ten days and complete with actors, costumes and music. The old caste divisions were lost, with much else, in the indenture system, but the polluting effects on Hindus of travelling overseas were still felt. These however could be mitigated, so it was held, by an appeal to Ram through *Ramayana* singing – in itself a purifying experience (Miller 2008: 96; Kelly in Sanadhyia 2003: 22). The Indian labourers, furthermore, far from home, could and did readily identify their own experiences with the story of the exile and sufferings of Ram, and his final triumph. It was not a matter just of private reading but of musical, social and religious activity.

The migrants also brought familiarity with many other musical forms with them. Principally these, like the migrants themselves, came from North India but there were many from the south too, resulting in manifold resources which they could and often did choose to activate in new surroundings.

These included above all the devotional songs, the *bhajan*s, sung in varying forms by both Hindus and Muslims. There were also songs associated with the ritual calendar, the most prominent being the songs for the Hindu *Holi* festival of social inversion and license - in part devotional singing, in part songs about topical events. There were the many popular songs of competition and insult too and the music for ceremonies such as weddings. But central to the weekly round remained, from the beginning, the regular *Ramayana* recitals carried out by local *mandala* (religious singing groups), together with the major religious festivals of the year all with their associated – and necessary - musical activities in which, at least in the early indentured years, Muslims and Hindus alike joined.

Drawing from these varied musical resources and constructing them in new settings did not, any more than music in English towns, just *happen* It took much organisation and effort. It depended on and grew from the commitment, ingenuity and musical actions of hundreds and thousands of individuals throughout the labour lines. At first it was difficult indeed for their was little sympathy for religious observance among at least some of the supervisors. Materials were often lacking too. Musical accompaniment could sometimes be nothing more than empty biscuit tins. But that could be enough. As Ian Somerville elaborates,

> 'Necessity is the mother of invention, and they hollowed out wood to make *dhol* (drum), *khanjari* (tambourine), and *kartal* (for beating time). A *tamboura* [one-stringed lute] was made from melons' – a tradition of using local resources followed in some Indian music ensembles over many later years, as with empty Fiji beer bottles struck as ideophones (Miller 2008: 95, quoting Somerville 1986: 98).

There was undoubtedly much that was violent and oppressive in the indenture experience of Fiji. In its initial years at least it meant the harshness of near-slave living and working conditions, and there was sometimes, as many realised too late, little choice behind their ostensibly free decisions to sign on. But the system had this advantage over slavery that some individuals were able to bring cherished religious books, song texts and musical instruments with them on board the ships and found some freedom to store and use them. Their musical memories and religious involvements came with them too, reinforced yet again by the continuing visiting and mutual influences between Fiji and India, one crucial factor in shaping and validating the migrants' experience.

Not that the music as it developed in Fiji was just some neutral handing on from the past. In Fiji and in India there was competition, even contention, between different movements within Hinduism. Visiting pandits from India pressed particular positions, sometimes using music to emphasise their individual religious messages.

Beyond this however the particular form of Hinduism that prevailed – the deeply devotional *Ram bhakti* (worship of Ram) - had a profound influence on Fijian-Indian music-making as on other aspects of their lives, the more powerful no doubt because of its protracted struggle for recognition (Miller 2008: 424). It set the *Ramayana* recital groups (*mandali)* and *bhajan* singing as central to their local culture, with a corresponding centrality to the music.

This was the more influential in that the Tulsidas version of the Ramayana used in Fiji was intended from the start to be sung and characterized by highly poetic and performable qualities (see Miller 2008: 163). In Fiji the link between Hinduism and musical performance came to be an especially intimate one. As Miller (2008) well demonstrates, musical performance became established as central to the Fijian-Indian religious practice, a highly participative activity.[21]

Amidst the manifold contributions to forging the Indians' musical experience in Fiji some names can be picked out. One was Totaram Sanadhya who came to Fiji as an indentured labourer in 1893 at the age of 17. He later gathered his recollections and published them in Hindi, giving us an amazingly firsthand picture of life on the lines, at the same time acting, intendedly so, as a powerful indictment of the system (it caused a sensation when published in India in 1914). He describes the singing of *bhajans* by himself and others, and the weekend playing of *khanjaris* (timbrel drums) and one-wire instruments, together with the *Ramayana* readings. After his contract ended he opted to stay in Fiji, marrying the daughter of a rich Indian farmer and becoming accepted as a pandit, educating himself to a high level through his own study. He became a leading member of the Fijian Indian community and was also in frequent contact with legal, political and religious circles in India. After his

---

[21] On this and other aspects of Indo-Fijian music and Hinduism see especially Miller 's truly excellent Chapter 4 (2008: *passim*)

return there in 1914 he became a disciple of Mahatma Ghandi who wrote after his death

> He was an ornament to the Sabarmati Ashram. He was not a scholar, yet he was wise. He was a collector of bhajans, but not a scholar of music. With his single-wired instrument he used to charm the people of the ashram (quoted in Introduction to Sanadhya 2003: 4).

Sanadhya's particular contribution to Indo-Fijian music was while he was still in Fiji. He was the organiser of what was probably the first *Ramlila* sacred drama to be held in Fiji, in 1902. He continued managing that for seven or eight years and encouraged similar events elsewhere.

Or again there was the Sanatani preacher from India, Ram Chandra Sharma, who spent five years in Fiji in the 1930s. An expert in devotional singing and the author of many *bhajan* collections, he used his music to propagate the *bhakti* version of Hinduism. He commemorated his arrival in December 1930 by a special *bhajan* on the theme of 'He who comes to Fiji from India'. In Fiji itself he became famous for his rendering of a favourite *bhajan* of Gandhi's, connecting the Fiji experience to Indian nationalism and to Gandhi's message of religious tolerance (Miller 2008: 115-22). He noted with approval the local singing from the Hindu *bhakti* repertoire, especially the regular gatherings for *Ramayana* recitals by *mandali* singing groups, the special *bhajan* groups, and the *Holi* festival singing. During his time in Fiji he had worked hard to extend these still further, encouraging the growth of *Ramayana mandali* in nearly every Indian settlement and according primacy to the recitation and performance of the *Ramayana* narrative.

Without the input and commitment of such leaders, and the determination and ingenuity, real if less visible, of many many 'ordinary' Indian migrants, the Indian music scene would have been very different. What was certain was that by 1937, with all its plurality, it had a very real presence in the musical soundscape of Fiji

Chapter 4 The media in Fiji in 1937

In the 30s there was a mix of media for conveying and realising music. Live performances abounded, central to the local scene but also with overseas links whether to Britain, Australia, India or Tonga. There were written texts and scores in European, Indian and (for some religious music) Fijian languages; gramophone records; radio. International linkages were also in place, with printed works, records, and radio presentations coming from many lands. Already too there was a flourishing international gramophone industry, not least emanating from India, and numerous radio links. In a few years' time, if not already, a contemporary observer could speak of how, even in 'once-sequestered native villages ... the radio from many an Indian store blares out the programs of half-a-dozen countries' (Coulter 1942: 15).

A new party in the scene, the 'talkies' too were already becoming popular. Cinemas were established in the main island; practically all operated by Indians (Coulter 1942: 96) and by the end of the 1930s were showing Hindi films based on traditional Indian theatre, dance and song and a focus for bringing Indians together in a joint imagined homeland culture (cf Ray 2004:

256ff). Fiji with its striking musical complexity and double diaspora of both Indians and, in a smaller way, Europeans was already no stranger to international connections and migrating musics enacted through the levels dally established media.

This then was the musical situation during J. B. Clark's 1937 visit: more complex doubtless than he and his contemporaries were aware of. None of the three 'traditions' were simple inheritances from the past – not even the Fijian genres, tied as many were to particular places and interests. Nor was it a matter of great swathes of music imported unmediated from elsewhere. Rather they were brought, created,, selected, and constructed or re-constructed by individual and group choices from criss-crossing resources drawn from, and partly shaped, by international channels of influence. In such processes Fijian musicians and their audiences were building and perpetuating their own patterns for yet further influence and participation.

The complexities of the musical situation were also moulded by the particular features of colonial government with its constructed division between 'the races' – as they came to be called. Thus was crucially manifested in the original decision to retain Fijian control of the land and a 'traditional' chiefly order, while

Indians were directed to industrial and commercial activities and (consequently – something the government and the chiefs failed to foresee) unprecedented opportunities for economic advancement.

From the London – and BBC – perspective the conceptual framework was the undoubtedly powerful forces of Britain and Empire. But for many in Fiji, not excluding the so-called 'Europeans', the nearer regional powers of Australia and New Zealand were also looming. So too too for many Fijians were the Pacific Island influences, especially Tonga, and, for Indians, South Asia.

The imperial setting was indeed important – and pervaded the motherland of India too – but *not* everything was focused on Britain.

PART 2. FIJI IN 1978

Chapter 5 Indian music, high and low

By 1978 the setting was different. The media
scenario had changed in multiple ways. Most
strikingly, Fiji was now an independent nation
(from 1970). So too was India. But the musical
situation was still multi stranded. Amidst the
plurality let me focus once more on the three
major traditions [22].

There were again, of course diversities, within
these streams too. Music-making was still a
matter of exploiting recognised musical resources
from many sources, drawing on these flexibly
and selectively, with some more popular than
others. As before, but perhaps even more overtly,
there were tensions within all three traditions,
especially the Indian and European, between the
high art 'classical' traditions and the more
'popular' forms often seen as 'modern',
cosmopolitan or urban – and thus, depending on

---

[22] That means ignoring important minority groups such as
Chinese, Rotumans and other Pacific islanders with their
own musical traditions, not necessarily the same as those of
Fijians.

the viewpoint, as either more valuable or more degraded.

So, once again there was Indian music, a sophisticated and specialised tradition interacting with more popular local forms.

Both ends of the continuum were well-supported in the Indian music shops by both instruments and recordings, (the established vinyl and the new-come cassette). Meanwhile the high-art tradition in Indian music was being strongly promoted by the Indian Cultural Centre (opened in Suva in 1972) who organised lessons in classic Indian instruments and music; some musicians had been to India for specialist training and a knowledge of Indian musical notations. And then, pulling against this from the more popular end, there were the songs and music from Hindi films. These were by now watched by large audiences in the local cinemas [23]. These were noted for their religious, historical and boy-meets-girl themes and, above all, their immensely popular songs, which also featured large on the local Hindustani radio channel.

Despite their basis in Indian classical music and religion as well as in western popular music some

---

[23] In 1951 many town cinemas were showing only Indian films (Mayer 1973: 190ff).

65

commentators saw these as contaminated – 'unfortunately' (B4/3) - by western styles and instruments and deplored their 'bad sad effect' on Fijian-Indian music (A1/8). The Fijian Indian press frequently condemned them as 'corrupting youth.. But this scarcely dented their popularity and the songs were known by everyone (Mayer 1973: 191), re-sung by local groups, and much played on the local radio.

Music associated with religious activities was still central to everyday Fijian Indian culture, both Hindu and Muslim. The *Ramayana mandali* had greatly increased in numbers since 1937, and sung *Ramayana* recitations with instrumental accompaniment of harmonium, *dholak* (Indian drum), and percussive instruments, were now a fully established feature of the Indo-Fijian soundscape, with recognised repertoires of tunes; the imported harmonium had by now replaced the locally-made *tambura* (single-stringed lute) (Miller 2008: 123). There were dramatisations in *Ramlila* and Telegu *Theruk-koothu* performances, all with plentiful music (Shameem 1978). Popular *bhajans* were sung by soloists, sometimes repeated by groups, often with harmonium, cymbals and drums, or in the *tambura bhajan* form that had come to be particularly associated with Fiji – solo singing accompanied by the *tambura* (one-stringed lute) (Miller 2008).

There were seasonal activities following the religious year too, often with lyrics taken from the original religious texts but sung to local tunes (A1/13). Singing was organised every evening for nine days during the festival of the 'Birth of Lord Rama'. *Diwali* had become an officially recognised festival, an occasion for musical entertainment, but *Holi* still attracted many *faag mandali* groups to sing the fast boisterous *cautal* songs of couplets delivered competitively back and forwards between two lines of singers. In 1978 there were sixteen such groups in Suva and Nasinu as well as one or more groups in most villages, sometimes with busloads of people singing together at the tops of their voices (A1/8).

Older Indian genres were still popular but sometimes in changed forms. The original Sufi *qaawali* genre, originally sung to the classical *tabla* drum had now started being accompanied by players of the *dholak* players, the popular locally made drum, and brought more into the style of Indo-Fijian *bhajan* singing. Some genres were being extended in new directions not only in specifically religious contexts but for general pleasure and life cycle ceremonies such as weddings or deaths: 'if there is any ceremony you need songs to go with it … I can't think of one ceremony where they don't sing' (Devakar Prasad, Deputy Manger FBC 1978, B4/5, 11).

Some was informal singing together with friends for relaxation in the evenings. There were also more organised Indo-Fijian societies making music for the mutual entertainment of themselves and others, building more, or less, on the established styles. Some groups practised and performed on a regular basis - names like the 'Empire Old Boys', 'Harmony makers', 'Gurus', 'Sharma brothers' or 'Geetangeli', immediately aroused interest and partisanship. These were male groups, usually of 5-15 men, amateur in the sense that their members mostly held other full-time jobs, but dedicated enough to their music to be practising 8 or 9 hours a week or more, as well as performing at the weekends for clubs, dances and weddings and, with the most successful ones, putting on their own shows three or four times a year and going on extended tours.

These were locally defined as 'Indian' groups, and their membership was indeed mostly Indian with a focus on Indian-derived music and instruments locally regarded as 'Indian' such as *tabla, dholak, sitar, tampoura* and harmonium. But they were also ready to use acoustic and electric guitars, drum sets and what was regarded as more 'sophisticated '(rather than necessarily 'western') orchestration and sounds – with PA, electrification, lighting, stage effects. It was sometimes a real mix of eastern and western instruments, bringing in a wide range from accordion, electric organ, guitar and bass to saxophone, clarinet and Indian flute (C1/1).

In practice they played many kinds of music, ranging through Indian traditional genres, Hindi film songs and 'European' popular music, this last particularly at weddings and other entertainments, according to the wishes of the audience. Groups could be quite heterogeneous: the popular 'Empire old boys' for example included Hindus, Muslims, Indians originating from both the North and South India, and a Fijian singer, and though some Indian musicians perhaps tended to be more conservative in their repertoire than Fijian there were also many new compositions. Some of the band leaders had taught themselves to read western musical notation (even held classes for their own members), but mostly the playing was self-taught and by ear, involving both memorisation and improvisationin keeping with many forms both of Indian and of recent popular music.

The guitarist Krishna Murti, a local bank accounts clerk, was one of the innovative Indo-Fijian players, inspired by a mix of Indo-Fijian, American, and classical Indian music and by the innovations of other local Indian players. He had founded and played in a sequence of (mostly) instrumental groups, often with some of his seven younger brothers –' Zodiac', 'Deltungs' (a name copied from an Australian band),

69

'Shadows' (again a copied name), 'Decibels'. He kept saying he would give up playing for his other obligations – 'but I couldn't leave music … I can't hold myself'. He was currently the leader of the successful 'Gurus', a band of Indo-Fijians playing a mix of music, the winners of many competitions, and prolific donors to charity. By 1978 they had put on 50-60 stage shows around Fiji and built up a fan following, a bank account and a large capital investment in their expensive equipment: guitars, bass guitar, electric organ, and drum set (still somewhat unusual for an 'Indian' group), as well as an Indian *dholak.*

Like many others Krishna Murti was initially self-taught. But he had also gone out of his way to acquire a remarkable spread of expertise. Coming from a family with an interest in music and in Hindu observance - his father a vocalist singing religious songs - he had begun singing and playing the mouth organ as a schoolboy in the 1950s. He happened to hear one of the first Indo-Fijians who played the guitar and managed to get a piece of wood to make himself a guitar with nylon strings, bringing it in to school to entertain his fellows and drawing six strings on his arm so he could practise in lessons! Full of enthusiasm he started playing with a couple of groups while still at school: the nicely titled 'Happy brothers', then the 'Jolly juveniles'. Not that either of them had lasted – the way of many youth bands - but it gave him the incentive to practise, watching other guitarists then locking himself in his room with his guitar and record player to try to copy them. At that time he was playing what he termed 'English numbers' and 'rattling chords on strings'.

But then he got a record by the American jazz guitarist Les Paul - 'so neat and clean and sweet' - and was fired to copy his style 'and more', then further inspired by 'The Shadows'. Encouraged by a local school teacher he went to classes in reading music, following this with a distance course on musical theory that he had found from the US School of Music (he tried others but found this the best), gaining proficiency in high-art European musical discourse. At the same time his own musical activities were steeped in the traditions of Indian religious observance. He used to pray while learning, and prayed regularly at the local Hindu temple, singing religious songs each morning and evening. Prayers before going on stage were part of the 'Gurus' routine and, with the occasional lapse, they avoided drinking for the reason that drinking would clash with their prayers before performance.

Although only part-time players - all were in paid employment - the 'Gurus' members took their music seriously, practising together three times a week and performing at weekends. Krishna Murti had not as yet performed abroad, but had played with musicians visiting Fiji and was making plans for a visit to Canada building on the Indo-Fijian network there where guitar playing had become popular. Under his leadership the 'Gurus' were performing light film numbers and Indian stage shows but also drawing on English, Indian and occasionally Fijian musical resources, including new numbers which Krishna Murti made up while on stage with the group ready to support him – but would then 'forget about it afterwards'. As Murti said, it was a challenge to apply his guitar expertise and the Fijian-European chordal style to Indian music, the more so that though a number of Indo-Fijian guitarists were by then performing, guitars were still thought of as 'Fijian' rather than 'Indian' instruments. To add a further twist he was currently studying Hindustani music and teaching himself the sitar from a book in English. Once competent he planned to electrify his sitar to add yet a further sophistication to his group. In few places besides Fiji, I suspect, could one find this kind of plural expertise in a practising amateur musician.

Chapter 6 'Fijian' music, an active local scene

Then there was what was classed as Fijian music, their musicians somewhat more ready than those in the Indian tradition to create their own new compositions or adaptations.

Here too there was a pull between genres regarded as 'traditional' and more popular 'contemporary' forms, though with more overlapping between them than usually explicitly recognised. The *meke* dance-song remained the classic chiefly-validated form, ideally still composed by the inspired *daunivucu* followed by the hard work of perfecting the combined group expression of words, music, and gestures. Older people deplored the claimed lack of interest by the youth, but polished *meke* performances were still on show on public occasions, with both old and new compositions still closely associated with the image and influence of traditional chiefship but also performed on other prominent or festival occasions.

The composing could take changed forms. A university student, herself a *meke* composer, explained that she thought of the flow of writing in which a *meke* came to her as somehow sharing the same inspired process as in the past. As before, group rehearsals had to follow.

But neither this style of rapid composition nor the generally conservative nature of the genre necessarily implied a lack of individual creativity. An example was one of *mekes* performed at the international South Pacific Festival of Arts held in Suva in 1972 where the composer had drawn on a wide range of materials, including Tongan influences, and in doing so had 'created his own tradition; his *meke* are notable for the number of different styles within one composition, as well as for changes of tonality' (Saumawai 1997: 354).

There were still huge numbers of choirs. Every village had a church with one or more choirs and there were said to be 100 in Suva alone, again predominantly Methodist though also some Catholic, Presbyterian and S.D.A. (Seventh Day Adventist). Given the large number of churches this meant very large numbers of people involved in music. Commonly choirs (both men and women) had 40-60 members, but some, like the famous Raiwaqa, Nabua or Centenary choirs, were 100 or more (Centenary had a roll of 180 with an average attendance of 100-120). The members were highly committed to this music-making, commonly practising for 2-3 hours twice or three times a week.

The conductor – usually a senior man, occasionally a woman - was very much the leading figure, with authority somewhat in the

Fijian chiefly tradition. They had to teach as well as conduct the choir, who, though some followed tonic solfa, mostly could not read music. Occasionally they used a blackboard but mostly the conductor had to personally demonstrate and teach each line (there was no accompaniment, not even a piano): as the leading choirmaster Saimoni Vatu expressed it they relied on the 'pitch pipe of me' (A!/59) - no easy task in the 4-part harmonies regularly sung by these Fijian choirs.

Primarily committed to sing in church, they also put on performances in other contexts.. As throughout all forms of music-making in Fiji in 1978 and later, there were constant public competitions so that choirs were constantly performing before judges and critical as well as appreciative audiences – occasions widely regarded as a source of fundraising (usually for some charity), raising singing standards, and generally 'having fun'. There were small competitions nearly every month, but the really big one was at the annual Methodist conference, where well over 100 choirs sang before panels of judges and audiences of several thousands.

The choral repertoire sometimes included, or was influenced by, *meke* singing but was largely inspired by European sacred music, almost always sung in Fijian and in a recognisably Fijian style. It consisted mainly of hymns, anthems and oratorio, including the continuing favourites of Handel's *Messiah,* Mendelssohn's *Elijah* and Stainer's *Crucifixion* where several choirs joined together for a big performance. It was a 'conservative' taste perpetuated not only by a deep love of such music but also by the limited availability of music in tonic solfa, and, especially the two former works which were by now regarded as a expected part of the Fijian choral repertoire.

There was also less formal musical activity, when people sat down to sing Fijian songs round the bowl of *yaqona* (the Fijian kava) or danced together to the accompaniment of a ukulele or guitar, often tuned Fijian style with Fijian harmonising (a lot of fourths) (B3/28). Older genres like the *sere ni cumu* bumping songs and *taralala* dance songs acquired new instrumental accompanying by guitars or instrumental bands.

More organised amateur groups also sang together, especially in the towns – around 30-40 in Suva, each with their own names – but also some in the villages. They usually began from some joint experience such as working together (like the 'Firefighters' or 'Cement workers' groups), sharing a particular background (members of one band had met in the leper settlement), or belonging to a specific locality (Bua ni lomainabua, 'Frangipani of Nabua', or

(Tegu ni Savu, 'Dew of Savura'). They then often forged close friendships, meeting regularly perhaps two evenings a week, usually with sociability and kava – typical Fijian setting for informal music-making. Such groups, and their music, were regarded as primarily 'Fijian': based on Fijian singing and harmonies, with relatively little instrumentation, and expressed in Fijian words.

There were others too, blending into these, who were adopting more elaborate instrumentation and greater performing ambitions, combining instruments like electric guitars, drum sets and keyboard, but still regarding themselves as Fijian and singing to Fijian words.

Yaminiasi Gaunavou, a farmer and an announcer with the local Fiji radio, was the leader of one such group. He resembled Krishna Murti (of the'Gurus' band) in his devotion to music but came from a Fijian rather than Indian background. Born and raised in a village he had started singing at school in the 1950s to mandolin, acoustic guitar and one-string bass. On leaving school he joined Radio Fiji, since for him 'radio was music'.

After work he used to sit around and sing with two friends over a bowl of *yaqona*, common with young men at the time. At first it was just for relaxation, singing old songs while he played along on the guitar. But then they became enthusiastic about the Beatles and the country and rock music they were hearing on the radio. His friends used the ritual Fijian ceremony of bringing *yaqona* to make a formal request: that he should try to get material together to make a recording. Two weeks later he had come back with Fijian lyrics for four songs and they then set to work together on the chords. As he later explained it:

> So what we did, we wrote the lyrics and sang to the tune of some of those popular country and rock music on radio. So we tried to blend island rhythm to country, western and rock … with a new sound, a new approach to Fijian music, looking at Fijian music as something to develop younger people in those days (Yaminiasi as reported in *Fiji Times* 28 Sept. 2008).

Word got around and new recruits kept turning up – 'one evening one new face, the next another' until seven young men were meeting every evening to drink and sing together, many of them already keen Radio Fiji listeners and aware of the styles of music then being broadcast. The number of songs grew too, eventually with newly composed tunes as well as lyrics, and they settled on the name 'Gaunavou' – it happened to be the leader's own name but was chosen because '*gauna-vou* means a new time, a new era and that's how we coined the word'. After several months' practice Yaminiasi was confident enough to ask the Fijian programme organiser on the radio for an audition. They went on a Wednesday, Yaminiasi recalled, and all their ten songs were accepted: they were broadcast the following Saturday afternoon with 'everyone at home listening, thrilled, so happy'.

'That was the start'. Yaminiasi's band grew and became formally organised, with its own bank account. By 1978 it had twenty-one players – including five of the original seven – all self-taught. It had its own (expensive) instruments and had broken with tradition in expanding the traditional acoustic guitar and ukulele into electronic sounds, including amplified guitars, bass guitar, keyboard and a drum set – with many of its members versatile enough to double on several instruments as well as sing. Not a professional band in that several members were in full-time paid employment and others in farming – several working Fijian-style on Yaminiasi's farm - they nevertheless had a full programme. In 1978 they were in great demand, with engagements most evenings for dances, parties and private clubs, and had done several more recordings for radio broadcasts – a procedure where Yaminiasi was extremely fussy over details, in keeping, he said, with his aim of raising Fijian 'to the standard of English music'.

Unlike Murti he had not sought any formal musical training and worked by ear, but continued to compose successful new songs, helped by his assistant Mosese, a clerk at the Central Planning Office. In time the group became what Yaminiasi referred to as 'a fully fledged Fijian rock band', and toured Australia, the Solomon Islands and Tonga. (A1/36ff, B2/24ff , B3/ 18, 20, *Fiji Times* 28 Sept. 2008 http://www.fijitimes.com/story.aspx?id=102069).

Yaminiasi's interest in composition was not unparalleled, for among all such Fijian bands there were many new songs, specially lyrics in Fijian but often the music too. These were sometimes composed individually but also by a group working together on both words and tune, perhaps line by line at a time, recording as they went on an audio-cassette. Or they might begin from a known 'western' tune, then 'find their own way' (A1/26-7). They also drew on international sources of popular and recorded music, listening to broadcasts, recordings, and audio-cassettes by other groups and memorise or adapt them to their own use. Underlying all this lay the remarkable Fijian ability to memorise and reproduce a tune, even after only one hearing, often independent of any reliance on written forms.

Chapter 7. European music, 'popular' and other.

These two broad traditions, the Fijian and the Indian, were at the same time intermingling with what could be termed the European musical heritage. This of course was the third great strand, charactrrised by all its diversities and the familiar arguments, known all over the world, about the respective merits of the many genres and sub-traditions, from classical through jazz and rock and more.

At the high art end the classic forms of music had some support from individual specialists at the university and teacher training college, most of whom had trained abroad; from the official Fiji Arts Council, who sponsored concerts by visiting musicians from Australia or New Zealand; and to a lesser extent in some schools. It was also promoted by smallish groups of enthusiastic individuals with their collections of records and access to overseas broadcasts from Britain, New Zealand and Australia. On similar lines there were recordings and instruments readily available in the shops. Some of these specialised in classical music recordings and in addition held a limited amount of sheet music and reading material.

There were also performances by largely European-based choirs and instrumental groups, mainly of operas and musicals – including, predictably, Gilbert and Sullivan (*The Yeomen of the Guard* was the one I saw) – held in such venues as the Fiji Arts Club and much approved by the local Arts Council. Some schools also put on shows in the light classical tradition, such as *Joseph and multi-coloured raincoat.*

The continuance of the classical music tradition to a high level was also dependent on local private teachers. Olga Parshotam, of European extraction, was one leading exponent. A Fellow of the internationally recognised Trinity College of Music she had trained in New Zealand and was now living in Suva, married to an Indo-Fijian lawyer. As a committed music teacher she was engaged in upholding the internationally-validated standards of classical instrumental performance and music theory. Following a similar pattern as in so many of the English-speaking diasporas across the globe, scores of the children of (mainly) European parents went in turn through her hands, successively undertaking the Trinity College of Music graded examinations, with visiting examiners coming regularly across from New Zealand.

The brass bands of the Royal Fiji Military Forces and the Police were another element in the scene. Working in the military band mould, with highly trained conductors, all the players were trained to read musical scores, and had practised familiarity with the European brass band repertoire - or rather with what had become by now the international repertoire (in fact the current army bandmaster had trained in India, spending three years at the Indian Military Academy for Music). They also played local arrangements including the-favourite Fijian farewell song *isa lei*. Like other members of the military forces, band players were Fijian (the army did not have Indians). By now band music, like sacred choir music, was taken as a fully Fijian (rather than 'European) form of music and always made a great visual impact as they performed in their colourful Fijian uniforms, complete with *sulus* (traditional Fijian men's skirts) on public occasions, often spectacularly playing in and out the international liners that regularly called at Suva.

The same in a way applied at the popular end of music, referred to in Fiji by the familiar label of 'pop music'. Musicians and audiences in Fiji, as elsewhere, kept in touch with international musical trends through local radio (pop music was prolifically broadcast (B2/12)), discs and audio-cassettes, as well through local performances and their own travels, when they sometimes proudly returned with the latest recordings only to find that they were already well known in Fiji. Most English popular numbers had equivalents in Fijian (A1/, were widely sung and felt – by younger people at least

- to have a local not just an international feel about them.

There were plentiful amateur 'pop groups' like the 'Nadro swingers', the 'Quintikis', 'Racial harmony' or 'Sangfroid ride'. These performed mainly at the weekends and for special occasions like weddings (extensively advertised in the *Fiji Times*) for a fee or expenses, using whatever mix of instruments they could muster, from guitars, mouth organs, bongos or organ to drum sets. These shaded into the so-called 'Fijian groups' mentioned earlier – after all there was certainly some rock influence in Yaminiasi's 'Gaunavou' band - and sometimes sang in Fijian. But they were generally thought of as part of the international European/American/Australasian popular music scene, often singing in English rather than Fijian or Hindi, and for their stress on instruments like drums and amplified guitars. Their members were primarily Fijian, but sometimes racially mixed – indeed it was in popular music that the racial divides engrained in Fijian politics were most often surmounted: 'English pop music' (so-called) was something they had 'in common' (B3/17).

Being up with the latest pop releases was particularly evident in the music for hotels and night clubs – usually live but also sometimes discos – where English was the common language. The full-time bands attached to local hotels and nightclubs were often more racially mixed than other groups, including for example not only Fijians and Indians, but Chinese or other Pacific islanders. Again mostly playing by ear they experimented with different styles, variously influenced by, for example, Bob Dylan or popular groups like the Beatles or the Animals. Some, like the 'Dragon swingers', 'Ulysses' or (currently the 'top' band) 'Lucky Eddies', were well known locally, usually singing in English to electric guitar, bass guitar and drums. In popular music too, as across the music scene in Fiji, there were constant competitions and 'talent quests', and as elsewhere experience in the local bands could at times launch one or more of their members into a professional musical career, sometimes internationally. In fact there was already a flow of players coming and going between Fiji, other islands in the Pacific, Australia and New Zealand (B2/55) – a Pacific rather than Euro-American centre of gravity.

There were also some notable jazz players, performing in a range of settings. The leading exponent was the Fijian jazz guitarist Tomasi (Tom) Mawi, famous for playing with his thumb rather than a plectrum. Self-taught he had been inspired in his teens by hearing the legendary jazz guitarist Barney Kessel and later Wes

Montgomery and tried to emulate their sound. By the late 70s he had played to great acclaim in just about every music venue in Fiji [24], and was widely recognised to be the leading jazz guitarist in Fiji and, by some, in the Pacific region more widely, even the southern hemisphere (by some years later he had, at least in his admirers' eyes, attained world-class status).

All in all there was a remarkably high degree of activity in the popular music sphere, organised locally rather than arranged or financed from some central organisation, and kept going by the efforts and interests of local groups and individuals, almost all self-taught and playing as much from ear and memorising as from notated music. The music they were playing was not just passively copied from the air waves. Certainly the musics coming from elsewhere offered resources and inspiration, but local musicians had to select and (in popular performance style) make their own even when singing cover versions or in English. Gaining an understanding of the musical genres they came to admire – through radio, discs, tapes, cassettes, films, live performances and (in some cases) school experiences – and learning the arts of playing was something into

---

[24] See http://www.manly.nsw.gov.au/IgnitionSuite/uploads/docs/program_flyer_aug29_v2.pdf//.

which they put great creative effort, suiting it to the audiences and co-musicians of the current local scene.

They were also playing within the particular media- and political context of the Fiji of the 1970s.

The mix of media and – equally important – their accessibility had greatly changed since the 1930s, not least because the Amalgamated Wireless (Australasia) Ltd (AWA) radio service of 1937 had now been replaced by the fully local Fiji Broadcasting Commission (FBC). This was not the only change. There were more literate readers taking advantage of print material – hymn books and in some cases notated music – and of the multiple local newspapers in several languages. There were the well-attended cinemas showing films, with their particular resonances for Indian popular music, and a multiplicity of music shops drawing their supplies from many international markets (among them Germany, France, Japan, Taiwan, Italy, China, India, Pakistan, France and the USA (A1/46)) with both European and Indian instruments, equipment, books, records, audio-cassettes and enthusiastic knowledgeable staff. Musicians and others now had the opportunity to get hold of a plentiful supply of relatively inexpensive discs and audio-cassettes were readily available for musicians to hear and assess opening new opportunities for musical explorations– in 1937 Krishna Murti and those like him would not have had ready access to recordings of overseas artists or been able to work from personally owned recordings in their rooms at emulating or adapting their playing styles.

Equally significant an industry in locally recorded audio-cassettes was starting to get going, complementing the earlier recordings from New Zealand or Australia and enhancing the profile of local music, making its broadcasting increasingly feasible. As elsewhere, too, these new technological opportunities in their turn were increasingly raising the awareness of the musicality of performance and non-notated genres in ways hidden in the older high art hard-copy scoring.

Radio continued to play a significant musical role, in many ways enhanced since the 1930s. There was at least one radio set in just about every home, even in rural areas – the transistor had come of age – and broadcasts from many lands were now in theory hearable on short wave receivers. Not that overseas musical broadcasts seemed to stir much general interest. The BBC World Service did continue broadcasts of various music styles: in 1978 for instance it was transmitting a modicum of classical as well as light classical music, together with some jazz, rock and a weekly half-hour hit parade (March 1978 schedule in *London Calling*). But it was attracting relatively few local listeners[25]. BBC reception had in any case been unreliable and both Radio Australia and Voice of America sent stronger signals[26], with the result that that the local station had increasingly been cutting back on direct BBC broadcasts, the more so that for most people English was at best only a second language. The local radio General Manager, seconded from the BBC, had summarised it starkly a few years before (1973): the BBC might attract general approval, but: 'all the goodwill in the world no longer entitles us to put out material which simply cannot be understood' [27].

Meanwhilec *local* radio had expanded and by now was widely listened to. At first it had continued to be run by AWA (Amalgamated Wireless (Australasia)). Over the years Beresford Clark had kept up a constructive and courteous correspondence with its Manager Frank Exon, and the BBC had meantime actively helped with

---

[25] In the 1969 audience survey only 4% of Fijians and 2% of Indians said they listened to it frequently, with Hindi speakers listening as often to All India Radio and Radio Pakistan (*Report of the Broadcasting Review Committee* 1970: Appendix 4: x. xi; this report focused on Fijian- and Hindi-speakers as the majority groups in the population).
[26] (GMTS Duty tour March/April 1977 p. 14, Media File, Fiji Broadcasting Corporation, E3/867/1, BBC WAC
[27] Media File, Fiji Broadcasting Corporation, E3/867/1, BBC WAC

'transcriptions' [recordings for transmission], advice, training opportunities, staff secondments, useful contacts and rapid moves to resolve potential disputes, encouraging and supporting the spread and coverage of local radio. [28]

By 1978 AWA had gone. Now it was FBC, the Fiji Broadcasting Commission – 'Radio Fiji' for short. Its grand opening in July 1954 was attended by the great and good, among them Beresford Clark who spoke in strong support and in praise of the departing Frank Exon and AWA (he also continued a cordial correspondence with the new station and its staff). Messages came from New Zealand and Australia - it was the New Zealand radio service that provided the necessary experts to get it up and going - and FBC increasingly operated in a Pacific-regional setting, now looking to New Zealand and Australia as much as to the BBC.

By 1978 then Radio Fiji was well-established and widely listened to (there was as yet no television), transistors now making it now vastly more accessible than before. As the 25th anniversary retrospect boasted, not without reason

---

[28] [E14/56/1 re letter blown away by gale 1959]

91

The phenomenal growth of radio broadcasting in these twenty-five years owes much to the cheapness and convenience and portability of the transistorised receivers that became available early in the Commission's life. They multiplied demand, both in volume and variety, for programmes to listen to (Usher and Leonard 1979: *This is radio Fiji ... 1954-1979* p. 27).

The scanty hours of 1937 local radio had been expanded into a two-channel service offering programmes in English, Fijian and Hindustani. These provided extensive coverage of local music, both Fijian and Indian, and the radio was booming. Still with some advertising, it was now a public service with all-day broadcasts from the 'Devotional' at 5.55 a.m. to close-down following the Fiji news summary at 11.05 p.m. (Saturdays midnight). In keeping with the 'three-stool' metaphor of three 'races' one of the two channels had now (from 1972) been allocated to programmes in English and Fijian, the other to English and Hindustani, so distributed that innSuva the English programmes could also be heard continuously on an FM channel.

As for their content: The English programmes had a high proportion of news and of informational material (including schools broadcasts), coming both from Fiji and rebroadcast from Radio Australia, BBC and Voice of America.. But there was also a plentitude of music: songs, light classical, band music, some folk and jazz, the early evening 20-minute 'Music around the world', and local productions like the Monday evening 'Hit parade of local artists' songs' or 'Music for you, with local guitarist, Sonny and George' (there was little if any room for high-art European music).

On Radio One this was interspersed with blocks of comparable material in Fijian (all originating locally), with hymns, songs, a considerable input of locally recorded Fijian music, a Saturday evening 'BBC pop profile' and a 'top hit parade' of Fijian songs, request programmes and the opportunity at certain times to send out personal messages.

On Radio Two, the Hindustani channel, the English sections were complemented by an even more substantial musical component from the Indian musical tradition – genres such as *qawali* (with a weekly 'local qawallis' slot), *geet, ghazal, bhajan,* Urdu poetry, wedding songs, a small amount of classical music, light music shows, a substantial proportion of film songs, and special slots such as request and message programmes, the weekly 'Music from Radio Pakistan' and a local artists 'hit parade'.

Nearly half this Indian material was locally sourced, the rest coming from overseas [29] while many of the Fijian musical broadcasts came from the resources of the Fiji Broadcasting Commission which by now had a highly regarded and growing recorded music archive. There were also live broadcasts by one or other of the local groups mentioned earlier. From 1972 onwards, there had in fact been a shift towards prioritising local rather than imported programmes and promoting Fijian and Hindustani as languages of equal status to English.

Settling this pattern for local radio broadcasts had not been without its problems. 1937-78 had seen the predictable arguments within the BBC and Colonial Office as well as locally about what type of music should be broadcast and about transmissions in local languages and cultures, notably complex questions in Fiji. How much music if any would be allowed in advertising slots? What *kind* of Fijian' language should be heard – was the so-called 'missionary High Fijian' more authentic then more colloquial versions, and if not which local version should prevail? [30] In the absence of available recordings

---

[29] This is extrapolated from the 1975 figures in *Fiji Broadcasting Commission Annual Report* 1975: 8.

[30] Just what counted as the 'Fijian' language was controversial given the many dialects of colloquial spoken

where would the broadcast Fijian music come from? How choose between the different forms and traditions of 'Indian' music, what performers should be heard, and how they wean Hindi-speaking listeners from All India Radio to a local service (Collins 1967: 146)? And in the familiar arguments raging as much in the BBC and elsewhere as in Fiji, what kind of 'European' music?

That question was much on the local agenda as the new service was being set up. A *Fiji Times & Herald* leader commented on the 'two camps':

> There is as yet no sign that perfervid jazz-lovers and earnest music-lovers ... are likely to meet on common ground. ...
>
> It is as well to remember that, although some of those who live in the Higher Cultural Circles sometimes lapse into arrogance in the matter of radio

---

Fijian. What could be termed the 'Old High Fijian', the missionary validated language, was for long taken to be the prestige language, used in church and thus highly influential in the early days of radio – but not necessarily acceptable to all listeners (Power 1995: 12). There were also arguments also about the local Fijianised Hindi: most accepted it as by now the standard, but some still stigmatised it as a 'degrading patois' (A1/12) or, in earlier parlance, an 'argot'.

programmes, there is equal arrogance among those who have a mental obsession over the term 'classical', and who shy like a restive horse from anything suspected of being in the category of worthwhile music (*Fiji Times & Herald* 2 July 1954, reproduced Usher and Leonard 1979).

As the FBC Manager put it, more temperately, at the opening ceremony

It is not easy to please all listeners all the time. But it is just as important that jazz lovers should have the best dance music as music lovers their sonatas or symphonies (K. G. Collins *Fiji Times and Herald* 3 July 1954, reproduced Usher and Leonard 1979: inside back cover).

The impressive music library built up by the Fiji Broadcasting Commission (FBC - Radio Fiji) since its foundation had helped to address some of the practical problems, – a wonderful resource for transmissions. It included BBC transcriptions – great source for classical music programmes - but above all a huge collection of commercial recordings from India, some dating back to the 1950s and before, together with material from All-India Radio and Radio Pakistan with recordings in multiple languages. Besides

Hindustani there were, among others, plentiful recordings in Gujarati, Tamil, Punjabi.

This already extensive archive had been significantly amplified by Radio Fiji's own local recording operations, principally of Fijian music where the main gap lay. Their resources were also expanded by joining disc-library organisations overseas to supply the FBC with the latest releases every month (Collins 1967: 150); by 1978 they were regularly receiving popular music discs from America, Britain, Australia and (to a lesser extent) New Zealand (A1/1). By the mid-70s they thus had an unparalleled collection of about 35,000 English records, 18,000 Hindustani records and nearly 5000 of their own tapes, mostly Fijian music (FBS annual Report 1976: 4).

But more than just in its broadcasts and its archive, FBC played an important role in stimulating and supporting music. Groups of local musicians were constantly to be found in the Radio Fiji studios, rehearsing for some event or working up to a Radio Fiji recording or live broadcast. The radio staff were enthusiastic and knowledgeable about music, both internationally and locally, and were closely in touch with the local musical scene, often themselves players. As well as encouraging those who came to them, they sponsored competitions − that recurrent pattern of Fijian music - and regarded it as part of their responsibilities to encourage indigenous music (A1/3) and go out to make recordings, specially Fijian performances, both already-scheduled events and ones instigated by themselves.

This also meant that they were a focus of struggles between competing musics. In April 1978 for example more than 240 Hindustani radio programmes listeners had presented a petition to Radio Fiji asking that priority be given to local singers and musical groups rather than to imported music and records from India (*Fiji Sun* 12 April 1978). A month earlier 'Radio bans lover's song' had attracted front page headlines in the local press when a love song had been kept off the air: the head of the Hindustani Programme had held that 'as a national radio station we have a duty to provide music of good taste and not the ones which are morally wrong' (*Fiji* Sun 9 March 1978). While in general emphasising popular music, the station also had to face regular complaints from those who would have liked them to give more emphasis the high-art forms, both Indian and European. But if always subject to controversy, in 1978 Radio Fiji was overall seen as a trusted and influential site and patron of music.

The political setting also had its relevance, not least for the local classifications of musics.

In this connection it must be recalled that Fiji was now independent. While still with many connections to Britain and the Commonwealth it was also increasingly part of the South Pacific region. Thus many musical groups looked to, and did, make performing visits to Australia, New Zealand or other Pacific Islands; Britain was more distant.

There had been other changes too. There were still residential, religious, linguistic and economic contrasts between Indians and Fijians, but these were no longer quite so comprehensive. Indians by now had an unmistakeable political and economic presence and there were now many Fijians in towns and in paid employment. People from all backgrounds, both from Fiji and the Pacific islands more widely, were mixing in the university – the University of the South Pacific now established in Suva - and both Fijians and Indians visible in many walks of life, their interactions more pervasive and multi-sided than in 1937.

But despite the new look brought by Fiji's independence in 1970, the divisions of 1937 remained. The earlier political balance had been retained, not least the assumption of Fijian paramountcy and political-racial separation was built into the constitution. The independence constitution solidified what might otherwise have been blurring distinctions by an electoral system based largely on 'communal rolls' by which every citizen had to register as a Fijian, Indian or General Elector (that latter including 'European', 'part-European' and the catch-all 'other'). The locally accepted term for the basis of this was 'race'.

The image of Fiji as made up of three racial 'communities' – the Fijian 'three-legged stool' – was thus enshrined in the new nation, and the distribution of powers perpetuated the previous prioritising of what were seen as the interests of native Fijians, the land-owners – in 'traditional' patterns, reinforced by the special position permanently accorded to the Fijian 'Great Council of Chiefs'. The divisions had been prominently symbolised in the Independence celebrations which exhibited songs and dances by 'Fijians' (that is, by 'native' Fijians), by Indo-Fijians, and by some smaller ethnic communities, carefully allocating equal budgets for the Fijian and the Indian portions (Kelly and Kaplan 2001: 131). [31]

---

[31] As all writers on Fiji have found, nomenclature is notoriously difficult here and whatever terms are adopted almost unavoidably carry unfortunate connotations. In Fiji itself the terms are often the tripartite racially (and politically)-based 'Europeans', 'Indians' (sometimes 'Indo-Fijians'), and 'Fijians'. These are mainly followed here but should not be taken as an acceptance of the racial and

In certain respects such distinctions did indeed reflect differing lifestyles and livelihoods (especially in the rural settlement patterns) and a range of religious, linguistic and cultural differences. Both Fijians and Indians learned much of their music in the home rather than school, to an extent reinforcing the patterns from the past and the more emotive for their connection with religious observance. Some Indo-Fijians felt that it was 'through music that they kept their culture' (A1/48), and as Brij Lal reflected on his upbringing in an Indian farming settlement

> The Hindi films, the Hindi music, the religious texts, the ceremonies and the rituals we performed with mundane regularity, kept us intact as a community. ... Hindi is the language of my emotion and prayer (Lal 2004: 247).

---

apparently solidified groupings they are sometimes taken to imply. 'Fijians' is especially ambiguous, since it can also mean all citizens of the Fijian Islands whatever their background (rather than, as elsewhere, one particular section among these), so some writers differentiate among them by speaking of 'native Fijians' or 'indigenous Fijians' - a practice I have occasionally followed to avoid ambiguity despite its potentially loaded overtones.

And it is true too that there was a general lack of sympathy between Indian and Fijian music cultures (the intermingling between Fijian and 'European' music was less fraught). As one observer put it, 'Fijians hate Indian music' a feeling that 'goes deep' (Mele Tuqota, B4 /28).

The racial divisions embedded through the political divides at the same time masked inner diversities, and were scarcely fully in accordance with the actual practice: the 'communities' of 'Europeans'; of 'native Fijians' and of ('intruding') Indians were artificially constructed ones founded in the political distribution of powers. There had long been areas of synthesis across the Fijian-European musical spheres; and the popular musics currently being played were to an extent shared right across what were otherwise projected as cultural divides. For one thing there was some attempt in the primary school curriculum to give pupils an awareness across the differing music traditions. Some Fijian singers furthermore had embarked on singing and studying Indian music (less often in the other direction, but occasionally). Such intermingling was real. But at the same time the political-racial classifications had an inescapable influence on local alignments and discourse, including in the labelling and practices of music.

PART 3 THE MUSICS OF FIJI IN 2009

Chapter 9 An island and a region in change

So now we have arrived at March 2009. This was when I visited Fiji for the second time, spent many hours in what by then had become the Fiji Broadcasting Corporation Limited [FBCL], and had the chance to observe, discuss with radio personnel and musicians in Suva, as well as keeping in some contact later through distance communication.

So how, by then, were the travels and travails of 'music'?

In some ways the situation was radically different from that in 1978. Politically there had been four coups and the country was now under military rule (soon to be further tightened) with implications both for Fiji's demographic make-up – in particular a large Indian exodus - and for music practices both within and beyond Fiji. There had also been a striking change in the range and variety of media - again highly relevant for music - and, amidst this, the musical role of radio..

We will need to return to these aspects, but let us focus first on a few individuals and the situation they found themselves in, touching on these new – yet also old – settings.

After the usual greeting at the international airport by a foursome acoustic band of guitars and singer in Fijian garb –pushing the image of the 'native Fijian-ness' and musicality of the land – one of the first people I spoke with was the Indo-Fijian Marshud Ali.[32] Born and bred in Fiji, now in his mid-thirties with three children of his own, he also had many relatives who had migrated overseas – in the US, Australia, New Zealand - with whom he kept closely in touch and who came back frequently. Now working as a taxi driver he was not himself a musician or with pretensions to any musical expertise. Nevertheless he listened to music a great deal. His preference was for religious music above all that associated with the regular music-imbued *Ramayana* recitals, the *Ramlila* dramas and the *Holi* festival singing. For him, as for so many Indo-Fijians, such music and its associations still had great resonance. It was something he had learnt not at school but from his grandparents, still living in the village where he was born. Second to that however he was enjoying popular music in radio broadcasts: not his first interest

---

[32] Based on personal communication 16 March 2009.

but, as he said, 'if you learn to understand it, then you must [come to] love it'.

In his low-key way, Marshud Ali reflected the musical interests and commitments of many of his Indo-Fijian compatriots, both in Fiji and abroad. Music.-making was still central to the practice of Hinduism in Fiji, 'an intimate bond between in the devotee and the divine', as Miller puts it 'notable for its participatory quality' (Miller 2008: 4). Members of local *mandali* singing groups were still meeting weekly to sing and recite from the *Ramayana,* sometimes joining together in more high-profile events. In late 2008 for example 25 groups from Suva and nearby towns had sung in turn at one-hour intervals to complete the seven chapters of the *Ramayana* over 32 hours, in prayer for (the much-longed for) peace and stability in the country. [33]. For Indo-Fijians the musical year was structured round the big religious festivals, principally the music-pervaded festivals of *Holi* but also *Diwali* and the *Birth of the Prophet Muhammad* (both now public holidays), now supplemented by more secular occasions such as Father's Day. Divided as they were among many sub-divisions and sects within both Hinduism and Islam, they still shared an appreciation of

---

[33] *Fiji Times* 14 Sept 2008http://www.fijitimes.com/story.aspx?id=100608.

105

devotional singing, of festival events and of the by-now lingua franca of Fijian Hindi.

Not that this continuing tradition or the broadly uniform patterns of *mandali* recitals with their repertoire of current tunes meant unchanging repetition. Singers learned from each other, heard recorded renderings, radio transmissions, web renderings and new songs both locally and from abroad. Film song melodies were adopted for *Ramayana* recitals. Visiting performers with different approaches from India and elsewhere added to the possibilities, and in devotional music too fashions could change. Miller describes for example how an Indian singer's Fiji tour inspired many local religious singers. As a local teacher, already an admired religious singer, responded to it

> For the last two or three years, I've been using some tunes that were sung by Ramesh Bai Oza, who is from India. When he came to the program here, he had some very nice tunes ... He had the program for ten days, in the daytime for six hours and the nighttime for six hours. I attended those all-day programs. His programs also run on the radio on Sundays, so we have been recording that also. ... It was quite difficult for me to learn those tunes, and I don't think any mandali in Fiji at the moment is using

those tunes because they're quite difficult (Sailesh Kumar, quoted in Miller 2008: 212)

As in 1978 there were debates over the virtues of Indian classical genres, still actively taught at the Indian Cultural Centre, as against more popular genres. The interest in high art Indian music had expanded since the 1970s, and light classical devotional forms still attracted a wide following. The well-known genres still flourished, *bhajans* with their festival and literary associations, *ghazal, kirtan, qawali* - but not necessarily with the same styles as in India or the longer tradition. New *qawali* songs were composed about topical events such as the 2006 elections, popular among both Hindu and Muslim performers (Miller 2008: 310).The shelves of FBCL's music archive included substantial numbers of local recordings under such headings as 'local qawali', 'local geets', and broadcasters tried to ensure that recordings from overseas were tempered by these local forms. Older songs from the 1960s and earlier retained their popularity, still in demand from the radio archive: these were the 'old hits' or 'gold' songs still much favoured on the public service Hindi station of Radio Fiji, as well as the 'semi-gold' from the 1970s and 80s, including light *ghazals*, romantic songs and *bhajans*. It put on a 2 hour programme every Thursday evening, for example, of 'Local Bhajans, Kirtans,

Lokgeets, Birha, Filmi songs sung by locals, and much much more'. The continuing interest in different renderings of devotional songs – light as well as solemn – came out in the Hindi radio stations Friday evening 'Kirtan parade'(*kirtan* being a responsorial leader-chorus hymn) where listeners voted for 'the top five Kirtan singers of the week'.

Among Indo-Fijians *filmi* – songs from Bollywood films - were immensely popular: a kind of parallel world to that of western pop culture but at the same time associated no longer just with India but part of an internationally circulating framework for popular music. They pervaded even the more 'traditional' airways of public service radio, with its focus on the older *filmi,* and featured prominently on all the – by now – multiple 'pop' Hindi radio stations and websites. The 'hot and happening' Radio Mirchi – the 'spicy' Hindi music channel on Radio Fiji that paralleled their '2dayFM English pop station' – brought the latest releases of Hindi film songs for younger Indian listeners as well as hits from the 80's and 90's, with some rock and reggae and English announcements mixed in with the Hindi.

They had stiff competition from other Hindi radio stations transmitting film music as well as broadcasts from Australian stations and All India radio which people could hear on-line. Radio Mirchi had been relaunched in 2005 to meet this challenge by making it 'hotter' and more responsive to listeners. It now had a big audience, mainly from late teens to mid forties, marked further by its success with advertisers who recognised the popularity of such-music-listening by an audience with high purchase power.

Such songs were not just listened to, but were drawn on and manipulated by local musicians. Bollywood tunes were incorporated into local genres. In 2006 tracks from a video CD of a musical stage show, this time from the Bhojpuri film industry were among the most requested numbers on Fiji's Hindi radio (Miller 2008: 409-18). They became immensely popular among Indo-Fijians, in part because something about their composition and rhythms recalled the way *bhajans* were sung in Fiji while at the same time appealing to young people with their fast tempo and romantic overtones. The melodies were drawn on and integrated into local *bhajans*, *qawali*, *kirtan* and other genres, as well as into local folk theatre and mobile ring-tones. They went on to attain a huge circulation among the overseas Indo-Fijian diaspora and there too musicians brought the melodies into their sung devotional repertoire.

As well as the many religious musical groups there were also in 2009 many bands playing what was described as 'Indian pop', both women and men.. Much of this was, again, inspired by Bollywood musical styles. Here too there was local flavour and bands often brought their locally recorded versions to the music shops and radio stations hoping for further publicity or the chance to perform abroad and/or take part as a backing group to a visiting Indian star. An example was the all-Indian 'Melody makers'. This had been going for about 20 years, mainly playing film music – some high tempo, some soft – together with some classical and western. They had performed locally, including backing an artist from India, and had made several recordings in the 'Hindi local audios' series produced by the SPR (South Pacific Recording) studio: 'Hits from film', 'Hits from Pakistan' and similar titles. The size had fluctuated over the years but had at one point reached 18 (including dancers), and many were still meeting regularly to practise.

Popular music was not just the preserve of Bollywood *filmi* and Indo-Fijian listeners. Take the position of Jokatama Qio[34], radio presenter for Bula FM. This was one of the six channels of the local Fiji Radio (now the Fiji Broadcasting

[34] Based on personal communication 18 March 2009, subsequent email interchanges, and further information on http://www.radiofiji.com.fj/bula-fm/

Corporation Ltd FBCL). It was designated as the 'Fijian pop station targeting the young, energetic and music lovers in Fiji' (meaning the 25-55year olds) and highlighting the leading local bands and groups in Fiji. Broadcasting primarily in Fijian, its motto was *naba dua ena sere* - 'Number One in Fijian music' -indicating a readiness to air new albums by Fijian groups, some of whom had given exclusive broadcast rights to Bula FM. They also played a variety of music. During the night when the programmes continued their live-streaming on the web both for local night-workers and for listeners in different time zones overseas, the emphasis was on gospel music, hymns, anthems, choruses and 'the word of God'.

Jokatama actively interacted with local musicians, hosting programmes for example to launch a leading group's latest album. Equally important he had close contacts with local recording studios who were quick to supply songs they thought would hit the market – they needed radio to promote their music, just as radio benefited from being offered free recordings for their programmes: a win-win situation as Jokatama Qio saw it. Some came from the local music shops too, eager to help their sales by promoting CDs over the radio. His network of local contacts encouraged local musicians to pop in from time to time, sometimes to provide CDs

111

to give away as prizes (and promotion), sometimes – though less often than in the 70s – to record in the FBCL studio: the week prior to my visit it had been a Fijian gospel group. Going out to record some of the many choirs and *meke* performances in the villages was not now so frequent but still sometimes took place: as Jokatama pointed out 'we go out to them – they can't come here'.

As a radio host he had to respond to the requests for songs which came in so plentifully by telephone, text and email from both Fiji and overseas - a notable feature of the local radio scene. So he needed wide expertise across the contemporary popular music currently sung and played by Fijian musicians as well as access to Radio Fiji's still impressive music archive and his own downloaded database. But as well as his commitment to contemporary Fijian music, he also, as he put it, liked from time to time to 'slip in traditional stuff to remind kids this is Fijian music' and even occasional items of Indian music, as well as drawing on old hits from an international repertoire .In the end, as he explained, the music closest to his heart was 'local songs - you know it brings back memories'.

This brief vignette highlights the more popular end of musical performance – the kinds of music broadcast and drawn on by Jokatama Qio in his radio work as by others on the Hindi stations, and heard by wide sections of the population.

Pop music of various kinds was clearly of great local interest for many players and listeners, especially among younger people. It poured out from multiple radio stations, buses, restaurants, shopping malls. The (secondary and tertiary) students surveyed in 2006 expressed a strong preference for 'western music', especially its 'lively beat', and within this the overwhelming majority favoured 'rock' and (even more) 'popular music' as 'modern' and 'up-to-date' (Tuqota 2006: 134ff). Much of this was recognised as having an international reach, with popular hit songs avidly listened to, downloaded and sung, and some radio stations listed the latest 'top hits' on their websites each week. The youth-directed 2dayFM station of FBCL for example subscribed to overseas suppliers and was sent music from the UK and US twice a week, specialising in pop music from 1997 on - 'the freshest and hottest hits' from 'RnB, hip-hop, rock, rap, pop, dance music and reggae'.

As elsewhere the current fashions had to an extent shifted from 1978. But not all was change – indeed it was striking to find some of the artists and groups of 1978 still performing and in demand – and the selective nature of people's listening meant that changes were perhaps related as much to differing age groups, districts and backgrounds as representative of some mass takeover by recent Euro-American globalising forms. Thus on the FBCL channels the English-language 2dayFM's 'fast and current' music was for younger listeners and popular with them, as against their channel of Radio Fiji Gold's for an over 30s audience with 'easy listening' music mainly from the 80s and 90s (and in the evenings from 70s and 80s) with country, classic rock, smooth jazz, soul and R&B. Similarly on the CFM stations (those of the competing Communications Fiji Ltd service) Legendfm concentrated on hits from the 70s, 80s and 90s, with only a smattering of current hits, directed to those who 'grew up listening to FM96 [their youth pop station] ... but now have reached a time in their lives when the latest rap music is getting a little hard to handle'; as against this FM96 was still perceived as targeted to an 'urbanised' population of 'westernized listeners under 25 years'.

Among the Fiji television transmissions a particularly popular programme was *Groove Thang*, a locally produced music television show on Saturday evenings 'a window into music videos from around the world as well as a chance to see what's happening on the local and island music scene, and directed to issues 'that relate to young people'. Differing languages and cultural preferences also had their effect, with many Indian listeners preferring Bollywood songs from various eras, many Fijian listeners more interested in rap or gospel.

And whether on the radio, live or heard from some other source, popular music as it was heard in Fiji was not just a reproduction of some incoming stream from America and Europe and/or (for some) from Bollywood, though that was very definitely among what they heard. It was also a matter of both listeners and active musicians using the many musical styles to which they had access to select among and play around with both within and outside Fiji. – and also, as will be evident from the earlier examples, and from Jokatama Qio's role, to have their local recordings and performances broadcast.

The styles summed up locally as rap and hip hop were currently particularly popular among many young men, especially native Fijians (Indians were sometimes involved but generally rather keen). Much of this now had a very Fijian flavour, locally composed and with Fijian words focusing less on drugs or guns – the interest in some other places - than on local issues in Suva and Fiji. They were about topics like politics and poverty and how the singers themselves were struggling, about nightlife in the local pubs and clubs, or sometimes about their hometown -

where they were born and where they were now (Soneel Ram email 15/4/09). The style, though certainly drawing on genres which had international currency, was something to make use of for their own songs. And there were singers everywhere. Thus in 2008 the Fijian rap song *67Ciwa Fiji* was for a time sung among the youth all round Suva's streets and buses, mixing English and Fijian words (*ciwa* being the Fijian for 9, thus cleverly making up 679, Fiji's telephone code).

Some held that there were fewer popular bands in Suva than in 1978. There was something in this – even if that is the kind of thing people always say (our familiar nostalgia for a supposedly richer past can be found in Fiji too!). There were perhaps fewer regular hotel bands, and recording studios had to a degree superseded some live night club gigs with a ready supply of disc renderings by local players. But there were still many local bands. But professional players still often started off as self-taught part-time performers in night club or hotel bands, often at tourist resorts, and there were many semi-professional groups for musicians to perform in, if only on an occasional basis, sometimes backing visiting artists from abroad.

The Fijian 'Jeriko' was one example, a band of 'Fijian boys and girls from Suva', played mainly in the pop, reggae, blues, and rock and roll tradition to English lyrics. Its make-up varied over the years – sometimes just a trio, but also often larger with acoustic guitar, keyboard, bass, drummer, vocalist and percussion. As one loosely attached member commented, his own upbringing in a musical family meant that for him music 'came natural, came to me when small, I love it, all my life, love music' (Sevanaia Tora A6). The fully-dedicated keyboard virtuoso was the son of Tom Mawi – that leading jazz guitarist from the 1970s and still around – with whom he had started his musical career and learnt, as he put it 'the skill of listening to what's being played by the other musicians in the band and playing my instrument in a way that complements them and the song'[35]. In various combinations they had been playing for some years at night clubs and hotels in and around Suva for functions like weddings and birthdays. They were now having success in tourist resorts in the west of the main island, had made their own live recordings, and been broadcast on local radio.

Many mainly Fijian bands were in fact playing in and around Suva and elsewhere, with no clear

---

[35] *Fiji Times* 14 December 2008
http://www.fijitimes.com/story.aspx?ref=archive&id=1089 14/.

division between what could be regarded as 'popular' and as 'Fijian' music. Mostly male, they often played just for social and relaxation reasons, relaxing with song and instruments round a bowl of kava in the evenings – still the standard setting - as an enjoyable part-time hobby rather than profession, coming up with their own rap songs. Many were young, some still at school (even some 11 year olds). Some groups were more ambitious. Their aim was somehow to find the money (or a favour) so as to make a recording, have it broadcast on radio or television, sell it where they could, and, for a few, to achieve semi-professional or professional success overseas.

There were constant approaches to the radio stations from groups with pre-recorded numbers, sometimes made in their own studios, as well as openings for bands to play in the tourist resorts where they had greater access to recording and marketing opportunities than in the more remote villages (cf Cattermole 2007) – sometimes with great success, selling large numbers of their recordings (the tourist shops in the Departures section of Nadi international airport were one important outlet, but Fijian discs were also sold in some overseas shops as well as on the internet). Competitions were avidly entered – still very much a part of the Fiji scene across all forms of music. There had been many of these in recent years, often with twenty or more entries from Suva alone, others from elsewhere. The winner would often get a substantial sponsored money prize (perhaps F$1000) or better still entrance to another contest abroad, hopefully to yet further success.

Local musicians were thus welding together their own musics, especially those with native Fijian or Fijian-European background. Sometimes they were working mainly in a Fijian setting, but sometimes also endeavouring to create a 'Pacific flavour' with their lyrics and beat - differently defined by different artists. There had been challenges to the established forms by musicians trying to turn established patterns in different directions, or with unexpected selections of instruments. Drums and keyboard were exploited in new ways, sometimes with a mixture of Fiji-based rhythm and English or Fijian (seldom Hindi) words – a kind of Fijian pop listened to not just locally but in live performances abroad and on the web. As one observer commented, players say 'lets try that' and 'have a go'. New experiments were encouraged even by some older musicians. Yaminiasi Gaunavou for example, the youthful leader of the 'Gaunavou' band in 1978 but now a senior media figure, was advising young musicians to ' live according to the time they exist in':

The style of music [now] is different. If they wish to make it successfully, they have to live within this period and try to develop something that some of the people from the past appreciate.

If they could blend some of the modern music with old music and come up with their own flavour and style, who knows, old people like me could learn to appreciate and love the kind of music today (Yaminiasi Gaunavou, 2008) [36].

There were many combinations – just as there are anywhere - and another favoured style was to employ the quieter rhythms of what was sometimes dubbed the traditional 'ukulele' or acoustic guitar playing, primarily by Fijians. For some this was a symbol of the 'true' Fijian style, shunning amplification and large-scale instrumentation. Part of the tourist image of Fiji revolved round this kind of music projection, well exemplified in the small trios or quartets of singer, drum and guitar and/or ukulele to welcome and farewell travellers in Nadi's international airport. It was also especially pushed on some of FBCL's radio channels: the

---

[36] as quoted in *Fiji Times* Sept 28 2008, http://www.fijitimes.com/story.aspx?id=102069/.

prominent image on Bula FM's web page (the station where Jokatama Qio worked) pictured a Fijian singing to an acoustic guitar to a background of palms against a sunset sky.

Players moving on to the professional or semi-professional circuit both within and beyond Fiji were usually drawn to rap rhythms. But in addition they also often developed their own unique combination of styles to suit their interests and audiences.

Daniel Rae Costello was one among the many examples of enterprising and innovative musicians. A singer, composer and sound engineer he had been born and brought up in Fiji from mixed Pacific and Irish parents, themselves both Fiji-born. Self-taught in music he had won local talent shows to represent Fiji in competitions abroad, sung as a soloist in night clubs and bars in Australia, then returned to Fiji to do the same with his band 'Cruzez' in the early 90s. By 2009 he had developed his own style of 'Aqualypso' (a blend of 'African, Island, Calypso, Latin and Reggae rhythms' as he described it), sung mainly to English lyrics sometimes mixed with a little Fijian. With this style of music he had toured widely around the Pacific rim – now increasingly the popular music frame of reference - set up his own studios and released over 30 albums, boasting up to 300,000 sales throughout the Pacific of his successful 'Samba' album [37].

Another was George Veikoso, now one of the most popular entertainers in Hawaii with a stage name of 'Fiji'. His style was what he describes as a unique 'fusion sound of classic reggae, Hip-Hop, r& b and jazz', sometimes with a touch of Fijian *meke* chant as well. Now an established singer and composer he came from a typical native Fijian background – church focused. His 'first professional singing appearance', as he put it, earned him $5 from the audience and 'the licking of my life' from his mother:

> Mom didn't want her 8-and-a-half-year-old son singing 'worldly' music. The only place I could sing was in church so every chance I could I'd sneak out. I felt in my heart that I had something (to share), and all I needed was a stage. I got on every stage I could to make that dream come true.

He later reflected on some of the musical processes and influences through which his music developed during his time in Fiji – clearly

---

[37] http://www.garageband.com/artist/daniel_rae_costello/; http://www.danielrae.com/index.html/.

already in touch with a range of popular music styles - before he left to forge a career in the USA:

Fiji credits three relatives with encouraging his interest in secular music and in shaping his approach to it. A great-uncle, Isireli Racule, who helped make 'Drums of the Island' a hit for Elvis, was an early inspiration. Uncle Sakiusa Bulicokocoko (of Bulicoko Band fame), was another.

Another uncle, Paul Stevens, turned him on to people like Stevie Wonder and Marvin Gaye, and groups like Third World, whose music 'was a melting pot of groove and feel'. Fiji mentions Earth Wind & Fire, Chaka Khan and Rufus, Janis Joplin, the Bee Gees, Parliament, the Average White Band and Tower of Power as other early inspirations.

Fiji's mother eventually bowed to the inevitable. By the time he was 14 he no longer had to sneak out to sing and was working with a Fijian band, Rootstrata.. 'That's how I learned to be in a group. Being in a group teaches you that you are one of eight guys who make this sound (together)' [38].

It was not always a matter of moving *out* of Fiji for professional music careers and there were also transnational performers for whom Fiji was a focus and those who, though not themselves born there, were nevertheless strongly attached to Fiji and participant in the Pacific music community of which Fiji was a part.

One was Michelle Rounds, a jazz vocalist singer/songwriter of 'Pacific Island heritage - Fiji, Tonga, New Zealand, Samoa' as she described herself, playing across a range of jazz, soul, r & b and Latin. She had started her public performances in Australia but in the mid-90s had chosen to spend over 3 years performing in Fiji before continuing her career from a New Zealand base and into the Pacific region more widely, still returning at times to Fiji. The attraction of Fiji was in part the chance to perform with other admired musicians, above all the still legendary Tom Mawi (the jazz guitarist already famous in 1978 Fiji) with whom she shared a residency at one of Suva's leading hotels, as well as singing

---

[38]Fernando Lobendahn, personal communication, Suva 19 March 2009; and
http://archives.starbulletin.com/1999/06/29/features/story1.html

with the resident band at the famous Traps Bar and at other hotels, night clubs, festival events and competitions across Fiji, and presented reggae programmes on local radio. But Fiji was already close to her heart. As she explained of her song 'Culture cross'

> I wrote about being half-caste, and the song celebrates the diversity of emotion, talent and life for people of two or more cultures – I love what I am and am proud of my white mother (English/Danish pioneers of the Rai Valley, Nelson, Aotearoa) and my coloured father (Tongan/Fijian/Samoan/European).
>
> I am a first generation Australian and am grateful and glad to be allowed to live in this great and mysterious Land of the Dreaming (hello to my friends in Broome!!), I love my mother's country of Aotearoa and have lived some years there in great happiness, but the country of my heart is my father's, Fiji - o Viti, noqu vanua dina !!

Her lyrics celebrate this,
> Girl in the middle, neither black nor white
> mixed   breed,   half-caste
> never   wrong,   never   right
> can cut it in society, can cut it on the street

she's just like sonny rollins' saxophone
long, hard and sweet

Chorus
culture
cross,   never   at   a   loss
adaptable, versatile, flexible and volatile
culture   cross
culture   cross,
never   at   a   loss
just coloured ... [39]

She kept up her friendship with Tom Mawi with
whom she continued to sing and appeared at his
benefit concert in September 2008. Though her
own songs were in English, some of her
recordings featured Fijian lyrics, like Yaminiasi
Gaunavou's Fijian love song *Era bini tu* and in
Fiji she was regarded as one of their own: 'our
globe-trotting jazz singer' [40]. The perspective was
not that of Euro-American pop but of the Pacific
region and the Far East.

In addition to this Pacific-wide circuit of more
popular forms, there were also still interests in
what were seen as the more 'traditional' Fijian
genres. *Meke* performances were still counted
among the classic Fijian genres (if with some

---

[39] http://www.michellerounds.com/index2.html)/.
[40] http://www.fijitimes.com/story.aspx?id=100595/.

haziness over just what nowadays counted as a *meke*). A strong attachment to this singing-dance style persisted even amidst its changes. New *mekes* were still being composed, sometimes primarily just to new words but also sometimes more radically, with changes in harmonies, style of singing, mix of voices or actions. These sometimes extended a 'contemporary beat to suit the [current] climate' (as Jokatama Qio put it) or additional instrumentation. Ukeleles and acoustic guitars had for some time been near-accepted as part of the *meke* tradition, but now there were also at times such instruments as big drums or what were labelled as 'Indian' keyboard sounds – leading to what was dubbed an 'integration kind of music' (Jokatama Qio).

Mekes continued to depict a story of some kind, in words, music and gestures. Some recounted local events, like the meke about a woman who went fishing on a Monday, left her children, and was killed by shark. But they could be about anything - sport, visits, ceremonies, and much else, including political events like the 1987 coup or one - still remembered - about the 1979 election (Tui). A 2008 competition laid down racial integration as its theme – a prompt from the military government. *Mekes* were still performed in public ceremonies and at such events as a feast, wedding, bazaar, beauty contest, school function, opening of a new building, farewell, religious meeting or sporting event; a special form (*cibi* – once the term for a war-song) was played before a rugby game to strengthen the singers' side and weaken the opposition. (Tuqota 2006, Tui 2009 etc). They remained a stock way to welcome and elevate someone, above all on occasions which were – or were projected as – in some way 'traditional': when a chief or public dignitary visited – or indeed a group of tourists - *mekes* were composed and rehearsed to greet them.

Perhaps there were fewer new *meke*s and fewer competitions than in the 1970s. The local radio archive by now contained many recorded performances so there was less incentive – and perhaps less money – to go looking for new ones to broadcast. But mekes were played every week on the radio – heard and remembered - and featured frequently on request programmes: people particularly favoured those from their own province but whether 'old or new, so long as it's *meke'* (Tui).

Their currency was also evident in the still-continuing competitions. A meke competition in 2000 for a group to represent Fiji in Florida had entries from each of 14 provinces, judged by a famous *meke* composer, while 2008 competition for new compositions had up to 15 groups entering from major towns (A8, Apakuki Waqa,

18/3/2009), regional events, and a major final to a huge audience in the Suva civic centre.

Most prolific of the active musical groups however were still the ubiquitous and characteristically Fijian church choirs. In Suva alone each of the many churches still had one or more choirs, and the same in other towns and the villages. People felt great loyalty to their own village and church, with its choir. Given the prevalence of Christian adherences, especially Methodism, among native Fijians a great proportion of individuals, were choir singers whatever their other commitments.

Leone Vuki, for example, an announcer on Radio Fiji One, was typical of many. He had a range of musical interests summed up on his official web profile as 'Gospel Music and Sigi Drigi (Sing and Drink) ... Old Hits, of course the 60's too!'. But he then went on to note his church choir singing. For him this was a personal constant. As he elaborated it in a personal communication, in 2009 he was singing in two choirs (tenor – 'and sometimes a little bass') one at his church, the other of junior choir leaders from around Suva: 'Raiwai Methodist Church Choir', and 'Group Choir – 1st District'. His choir was currently practising to lead the new month church service on the coming Sunday. As with many Fijians, religion with its singing was a significant dimension of his life. 'That's wonderful to be part of these [choirs] because I believe from the bottom of my heart...once we finished these life there was life after these life and to be part of heaven's choir ... have faith in the Lord, one day we will sing together in heaven'.

Choir competitions were even more prevalent even than those for *mekes*. Some were famous throughout the country, brought together and assessed in public judging. Every August the Methodist church (the largest Christian denomination with its members nearly a third of the country's population), held its annual conference preceded by a week-long choir competition entered by some hundreds of choirs (over 500 in 2008) with thousands of people from all over Fiji attending.

Some choirs had built up country-wide reputations. The Centenary Methodist Church choirs, already famous in the 1970s, kept their pre-eminent role, thrilling audiences and congregations (including myself) with the sonorous and even-toned exposition typical of this style of singing. Many choirs had also toured overseas with plentiful recordings of their performances, singing in Fijian both in Fiji and abroad. Gospel groups had grown out of the same tradition, many singing locally but again touring abroad and recording their own albums, with a deep engagement in their religious import. The family group 'Akafa Gospel' for example had since 1995 recorded four albums of gospel songs in Fijian composed by their father Pastor Jitoko Akafa. They had toured Fiji and Australia 'preaching the gospel through their songs ... a great blessing in the lives of the people' and in typical Fijian pattern had won the 1997 competition for the best Gospel Song of the year.[41]. It is worth repeating that hymn singing with all its variations had long been no external intrusion but a well-recognised genre of Fijian musical tradition, something with strong religious not just musical overtones – a 'spiritual' invitation.

In somewhat different style, but still regarded as an essential strand in Fiji's music, was the national military band, still with their full involvement both in the classic band tradition and its Fijian incorporation. Still called the RFMF band (the letters no longer meaning 'Royal' but now the 'Republic' of Fiji Military Forces), they were called on prolifically to perform for both public and private occasions and, unsurprisingly perhaps during a period of military rule, had been flourishing in recent years. The military band now had over 50

---

[41] Cover note on 'the best of the Akafa family Gospel CD, Procera 2006 NLCD 2693.

members and were recruiting more, as well as refurbishing their band rehearsal room and planning their own recording studio. The Suva based band worked under their full-time bandmaster Captain Lai Kamani – Suva-born and bred but musically trained in New Zealand – with some members at any one time assigned as band-players with Fijian forces serving abroad. Primarily a (native) Fijian band – as before there were no Indian members – their priority was to perform on official ceremonial occasions, making an impressive visual as well as musical spectacle, but they also appeared at festivals, fund-raising events and private occasions like weddings and dances. Smaller groups within it played on some occasions – a 20-strong jazz band, a dance band, a choir and a *meke* group. As before they had the musical training – all read music - to play from the established band repertoire together with Fijian songs and hymn tunes. A recent arrangement of 'Abide with me' was by their current bandmaster: as he said with heartfelt emotion, this made something new and touching of a tune people thought they had heard many many times already.

These military and police groups were demonstrably made in the European band tradition, but in other ways the kind of classical music associated with the western high art tradition had somewhat diminished in influence –

as had the number of 'European' long-term residents in Fiji. Sheet music was no longer readily obtainable and the external classical music examinations which featured in the 1970s had lapsed with the departure of Olga Parshotam to accompany her Indo-Fijian husband after one of the coups (personal communication 16 March 2009).

The scintillating performances being put on in 1978 in the then dignified Fiji Arts Club building seemed by now past and the building had become merely a barn-like locale for leisure activities. Some were struggling to maintain or revive a modicum of music teaching on the classical model but it featured only minimally in secondary or higher education, and music had become an optional subject in the school curriculum, often omitted.

On the other hand many were acquainted with western classical music, some indeed highly qualified in its intricacies. There were specialists in the university and institutes, often with their own choirs and collections of recordings, and perhaps listening with pleasure to performances over the web or on overseas radio, including the BBC (though complaining about its scant offering of serious music).

A notable classical group was the Fiji Arts Club Choir, so let me introduce their conductor. Robin

Palmer [42] was a consulting engineer originally from England who, married to a Fijian, had lived in Fiji for 22 years. His commitment was to classical music in the European tradition, consonant with his initial training as a chorister in Bury St Edmunds Cathedral and later experience singing under leading conductors in the famous Birmingham CBSO Choir. Now settled in Fiji, he had revived the Fiji Arts Club Choir in 1992 after a lapse of many years, first to record a programme of Christmas music for the Radio Fiji in 1992, and by 2009 conducting an active programme of regular singing and recording. He had close contacts with the media and the choir was well connected into the local networks, singing at Christmas in the Anglican cathedral, and working particularly closely with Fiji Television for whom it had recorded over 30 programmes. As for Robin Palmer himself – it was clear both in the enthusiasm with which he talked and, equally, in his total immersion in the music while working with the choir, that his heart lay in his music - in his leadership and joint participation in the choir and in conveying it to others.

---

[42] Based on personal oral and written communications March 2009, emails (various dates), disc of Fiji Arts Club Choir Christmas performance (FijiTV) 25 Dec. 2008.

The choir's singing and repertoire were largely (though not exclusively , especially in their famed Christmas performances) in the English choral tradition. Over the years since its revival in 1992 it had perfornpmrd a variety of music: from the ever popular Gilbert and Sullivan songs or selections from shows by Rogers and Hammerstein, to Easter and Christmas music and full-scale works like Stainer's *Crucifixion,* Mozart's *Requiem,* Haydn's *Nelson Mass* and Fauré's *Requiem* together with some works composed specially for the choir. But it was prepared to draw its performances from the music of many lands and also accustomed to singing in Fijian - its rendering of the Fiji National anthem (in Fijian) closed the television Fiji One programmes for the day and for some time it was they who sang the famous Fijian farewell song *Isa Lei* each evening.

The choir was in fact a notably multinational one. In 2009 its 40 or so members were from Fiji, Tonga, New Zealand, Australia, Korea, China, England, America, Canada and France– 'all', as the conductor put it, 'working hard together to produce music to the best that they can, all without any problems at all'. Its membership was somewhat fluid as overseas singers came and went on short contracts, but by 2009 the nucleus was local, principally native Fijians and long-resident 'Europeans' (there was little if any

135

involvement from Indo-Fijians). Not all were fluent in reading notated music, but native Fijians were of course no foreigners to the skills of memorising, of beautiful singing, and of performing across many genres, and provided some wonderful soloists for the choir.

In 1978 such a choir would have contained mainly 'European' members and presented staged performances in the Fiji Arts Club building – that no longer happened. But with their televised appearances they were in fact reaching wider audiences than had been possible in the past. Christmas 2008 for example saw a well-rehearsed hour-long [?] television production by the choir, starting with the solo first-verse of 'Once in Royal David's City' – traditional to English choral Christmases – and continuing through well-known carols in English, Latin and French interspersed with English-language Christmas commentary by a Fijian presenter.

The high art western music tradition may have been less overtly revered than it earlier years but it still had its influence, specially in its long interaction with Fijian singing, brass bands and local church music. There were various projects from time to time drawing explicitly on the combined resources of Fijian and western classical music. In 2009 an adaptation of Bizet's *Carmen* was being worked on by a classically trained Fijian musician, Igelese Ete, together with *meke* composer Damiano Logaivau. The plan was, as Igelese put it, 'to Fijianise or Pacifikise' it as *Domo ni Karmen*, 'Fiji's first Pacific opera'. The singing would come from his choir 'Pasifika Voices', most of whom – typical of Fiji - sang in their local church choirs or were self taught [43].

It was clear then that there had been many changes and innovations since 1978. From the more conservative church music styles or meke genres, the ever-popular Messiah or Gilbert and Sullivan songs, or the complex blend in military bands and singing groups of what would have been separately classified as European and Fijian musics but now often sat well together, to the development of 'Pacific' styles, Indian locally moulded hymns or the Fijian shaping of hip hop and popular song, innovation and admixture ran through music-making in Fiji. In all these dimensions and more the situation was heterogeneous, a multisided set of flexible tools well exploited by the many Fijian performers both in the islands and abroad.

In terms of 'the travels of music', one feature of the Fijian musical scene in 2009 was the interaction between what might once have been

[43] *Fiji Times* 29 March 2009
http://www.fijitimes.com/story.aspx?id=117979/.

separately classified as originating in Europe, in Fiji or in India respectively. Much was now simply the music of and in Fiji. There were differences indeed between genres and their adherents, and between high-art and popular forms, the former being still sometimes validated by their (supposed) historic origins, the latter with both local and international dimensions. But by 2009 it was more just a matter of a range of musics being played and enjoyed within Fiji.

The absence of separately attributed origins, whether perceived and actual, was most striking between what would once have been differentiated as of 'western' and of 'Fijian' origins but by now fully a part of Fiji's soundscape - in religious music, choirs, bands, popular groups and more. Nor did even the somewhat more distinct 'Fijian' and 'Indian' music exist in totally separate spheres. Most people had some familiarity with music across the board, and often sang along in the buses whether the popular songs being played on the radio were Fijian, Hindi or English. Indians as well as Fijians were Methodist, if in small numbers, Indian keyboard sounds were heard even in *meke* performances, and Jokatama Qio aptly referred to an 'integration kind of music' and 'Fijian remixes' where one verse of a song was sung in Fijian, one in Hindi. Indo-Fijians as well as native Fijians now sat round a kava bowl for informal singing.

There was also a degree of fusion in dance, where to the same Fijian music native Fijians and Indo-Fijians danced simultaneously, each with their own costume and dance style (the Indians dancing 'in an Indian way' as it was put), sometimes further adding 'Pacific Island movements' from Tonga or Samoa (Miri A2, Tuqota 2006: 149).

There were also a number of Fijians singing Hindi songs, both religious and 'Indian pop'. As in 1978, this was a practice that several people noted with pride; it was also promoted by the local music industry through recordings and sponsoring competitive stage performances.

One example (reported in Miller 2008: 371ff) was the Fijian Juniya Noah, a singer of both popular Hindi film songs and devotional songs. He had grown up in a small Fijian village but from an early age attended the weekly *Ramayana* recital in a neighbouring Indian settlement from which he learned to sing from the Indian religious repertoire. As well as teaching himself to play the harmonium and several types of drum, he learned to sing a cross-section of Indian traditional genres (*bhajan, lok geet, ghazal, qawali, kirtan*), becoming popular among Indo-Fijians and even successfully entering local *bhajan* competitions. He also chose to immerse himself in Hindu religious tradition and sing at Hindu ceremonies, performing in an Indian rather than indigenous-Fijian vocal style so that, as he put it, 'if you put me on a cassette and played it for an Indian guy, he'd never know that a Fijian guy was singing' (quoted Miller 2008: 373).

Such instances were impressive in personal terms and in other settings might well have been the precursor of further integrated styles. But it was interesting that in Fiji no fused Indian-Fijian genre had emerged as it had in the Caribbean. Despite cases of Fijians performing from a Hindi repertoire – some of them high-profile - there was nothing like the Trinidadian chutney, the Indian-Caribbean genre that melded together musics from multiple roots (see especially Ramnarine 1996). Juniya Noah did indeed adopt a Hindi repertoire and performance style, but he brought nothing noticeably 'Fijian' to his music nor was he forging the creation of any new cross-over genre.

Indeed local classifications seemed to insert a clear division between 'Fijian' and 'Indian' music. Juniya Noah was held up not as creating a new fused style but as – counter intuitively it seemed – a 'Fijian' singer of 'Indian' music. Such a separation, as we have seen, went back a long way in Fiji, solidly established in political and racial classifications. It was further institutionalised in the carefully measured threefold English/Fijian/Hindi division of channels within Radio Fiji: a matter not just of linguistic divisions but also, very explicitly, of music: not just its styles but its target audiences.

Porous as in some ways the distinction was, this labelling of 'Fijian' as against 'Indian' music had formed one continuing thread in the musics of Fiji, validated as it apparently had been by actual or constructed linguistic, cultural and political divisions. But by 2009 the divisions had been notably intensified by political developments over the last 20 years. Since 1987 there had been a series of coups (1987 (2), 2000, 2006, 2009(?) − four or four and a half, depending on just how you count them - with dislocation of governmental institutions, censorship of the media and increasing control by the military which still dominated government at the time of my visit in March 2009 and was further strengthened during subsequent months.

The propelling factors were more complex than just a struggle between Indians and Fijians, for they also interacted with local, religious, business and individual conflicts (see e.g. Trnka 2009), but they were certainly seen by many in those terms and, more specifically, as designed to ensure continuing political control by native Fijians and traditional chiefs against any possible takeover – elected or otherwise – by Indians. Among the results was undoubtedly an intensifying of ethnic rhetoric, made use of by many parties to the conflicts, and, in 2000 in particular, extreme violence against Indians in many parts of Fiji.

The military government of 2009 spoke about 'racial integration' but the successive coups had in fact been widely experienced as driving a further wedge between Fijians and Indians. They had overall resulted in a greater self-consciousness about the boundaries between the two – permeable though these were in many individual instances. Ultra-nationalist Fijian rhetoric and taukei movements had urged the Fijianisation of local institutions with a vision of reclaiming Fijian control of the country from the threat posed by intrusive grasping Indians; the aspiration was to reclaim 'Fijian people's position and rights in their country of heritage ... eroded ... [and] threatened by a non-indigenous takeover', as it was articulated in Asesela Ravuvu's *The facade of democracy,* where 'Fijians... must be assured of a degree of political paramountcy, if all races are to live together peacefully' (Ravuvu 1991: 98-9).

On the other side was the Indo-Fijian view, less vociferously expressed but deeply felt, that it was they whose work had created the wealth of Fiji and developed its land unlike, even in spite off, members of the lazy and uncivilised indigenous population. The polarising was further intensified by the episodes of extreme violence against Indians during the 2000 coup (documented in Trnka 2008). Most people in Fiji, whether native Fijians or Fijian Indians, probably did not in most contexts take up either of these extreme positions. Nor did such rhetoric have a clear one-to-one relationship with music. Nevertheless it was part of the scene and one set of vocabularies that could strike a familiar bell even among those to whom such dichotomies were not in all respects acceptable.

The separating of Hindi and Fijian music had not been swept away by the huge extension in the range and variety of media for music. Nevertheless the proliferation of media since was of some relevance for musical integration or, at least, mutual understanding, especially in the popular music arena. The changed and changing media context in one way offered greatly enhanced opportunities to people to both hear and practise a wider variety of music, and a potential bridge between differing musical experiences, accessible across an international context. At the same time it both reflected and helped to shape the labelling – and experience – of musical genres.

In 1978 the main media picture had consisted of one local radio station – influential patron of local music – and a series of accessible international stations for those with the right equipment, together with a flood of gramophone records and audio-cassettes, both local and from overseas, films, musical resources in hard copy form (written text, notated or solfa), and, of course (if in a slightly different sense of 'media'), people's musical memories and the plentiful settings for live performance.

Most of these were still there in 2009 – there was no radical sweeping away of the past. But their relative significance had altered and there were also new players in the field. Sheet music on the western pattern was even harder to come by than in the 1970s (surreptitious photocopying to an extent filled the gap and solfa versions continued to be prized) and the once-dominance of film in the moving image medium had been partly undercut by alternative visual channels, thought there was still a cinema in Suva putting on an alternation of English-language and Hindi films. Recently announced plans for two Bollywood productions to be partly filmed in Fiji had stirred great interest, one to be the first Fiji-Hindi musical comedy with the nice title of *Pump up the Mandali* about four underprivileged boys who realise their dreams to be successful musicians after winning an international musical competition[44].

There were also additional forms – altogether by 2009 a huge mix of media. There was now a multiplicity of radio stations. Television, absent in 1978, was now established as the corporate Fiji Television, covering both a free-to-view service (Fiji One) and pay TV as SKY Fiji in Fiji and SKY Pacific for the Pacific region. Fiji TV transmitted many films and other programmes fro abroad but also engaged in recording and transmitting local musical performances both from Suva and to some extent from more remote villages, often organised specifically for television broadcast. Videos, CDs and DVDs supplemented audio-cassettes and old-style discs, with Ipods and MP3 popular among the youth. With Vodafone as the monopoly local provider just about everyone had a mobile phone, some with radios built in, and were ready to download ring tones from their favourite music or send text requests for particular songs. For some, especially in the towns, the internet was yet another resource for hearing and discussing music (up to a point: within Fiji where internet access was probably only around 10% among the

---

[44] *Fiji Times online* 5/5/09
http://www.fijitimes.com/story.aspx?id=120759

145

population as a whole – but much used, and in creative ways, among the Fijians abroad). Equally notable had been the proliferation of local recording studios, by now a key element in the local musical scene. They had expanded from the earlier audio-cassette recordings (though these were still in currency) to CDs and DVDs, and were endeavouring to publicise and market their wares both locally and overseas and, increasingly, on the web. [45] The changes in the media resources interacted with people's perceptions and experiences of music to set a different scene from 1978.

It is worth elaborating further on radio, for amidst the mix of media it was arguably radio that remained the most influential, though the details had of course changed. International stations were accessible for those who wished to listen (though those with local transmitters had sometimes been jammed in turbulent political

---

[45] e.g. SPR (South Pacific Recordings Ltd) in Nadi (plus small branch in Suva) http://www.sprfiji.com/sprbody.htm/; Daniel Rae Costello in Lautoka organising production and marketing of his own and others' performances http://www.garageband.com/artist/daniel_rae_costello/ and generally http://www.google.co.uk/search?q=recording+studio+suva &ie=utf-8&oe=utf-8&aq=t&rls=org.mozilla:en-GB:official&client=firefox-a/.

times), including the BBC and broadcasts from, for example, America, China, Germany, Australia, New Zealand, and of course India. With transmission via satellite people no longer needed short wave sets and good aerial to listen (indeed the BBC was available on FM radio – not that it by then seemed to carry very much music that people wanted to hear) and several international stations were available in live streaming on the web.

Local radio had a wide audience. With its major focus on music it was listened to by all sections of the population throughout Fiji – and for long periods at a time. Many many more people had access to radio than to television or the internet, and radio was a resource – relatively cheap and simple – that could be found in just about any setting. It was played on buses even when this was in theory forbidden, and people often sang along, whatever the type of music (Miri B p.8,, Susanna Trnka 2008). Radio was a readily accessible and popular medium– one reason why the commercial stations were able to sell their advertising slots so effectively – and its musical offerings widely heard both attentively and as background, with a major role in both the reflection and formation of differentiated local musical tastes.

The Fiji Broadcasting Commission of the 1979s had now transmuted into the Fiji Broadcasting Corporation Limited [FBCL], corporatised in 1998. This remained the leading radio service with its 6 stations, two in each of the three major languages (English, Fijian, and Hindustani (Hindi), each with their own targeted markets, musical styles and live streaming on the web (http://www.radiofiji.com.fj/index.php). The government bought time on Fiji Radio 1 (Fijian) and 2 (Hindustani), their income supplemented by advertising, while the other four were commercial. Music featured predominantly on all these stations, especially the commercial ones, each with their target audiences. As the two 'public' stations Fiji Radio 1 and 2 had a somewhat higher proportion of talk but relatively conservative music, while of FBCL's commercial stations Radio Fiji Gold (English) was 'easy listening', Bula FM (Fijian) and Radio Mirchi (Hindustani) the 'vernacular pop stations', and 2Day FM as 'our youth English station' Locally performed or composed music featured on all stations (even to an extent 2DayFM).

FBCL was the largest service and had near universal coverage, including transmission through the widespread mobile phone network; It also had the great advantage of its huge music archive, with its vast collection of local recordings, especially of Fijian music, as well as its international resources. It could mount block music programmes at the weekends and satisfy almost any request from its listeners. Indeed as the FBCL director of music explained they were the only institution that could 'play old songs that were recorded from the late 60's which we have now because we were the only radio station at the time, and we were recording all the local songs here then' (Asaeli Ratuwara email 1/5/09). As it stressed to its potential advertisers – essential for their financial survival – their local audience was not only 'media and tech savvy', but 'loves music'.

There were other local radio stations too, in all of which music was central. Communications Fiji Ltd (CFM), now a South Pacific broadcasting company, had started off as the first private commercial radio station in Fiji in the early 1980s and now boasted 5 radio stations in Fiji[46]. They too had separate outlets for the three main languages in Fiji and differentiated themselves in terms of their style of music and projected audiences: FM96 with 'the hottest music' for 'westernized listeners under 25', Legendfm for 'hits from the 70s, 80s and 90s' for those who 'have now reached a time in their lives when the latest rap music was getting a little hard to

---

[46] http://www.cfl.com.fj/.

handle', VitiFM for the 'traditional Fijian market' with more talk but also 'great music', the Hindi Navtarang with a Bollywood style and music/personality based format, and, for the 'more conservative end of the Indo-Fijian market', there was Radio Sargam.

Among the large number of fast-proliferating smaller stations were Mix FM transmitting English songs in the west of the main island [?], and the Hindi and English BulaNamaste FM, also dubbed 'India from Fiji' (the name combines the Fijian and Hindi terms for greeting), based in Suva but also hearable on the web playing Indian music described as 'Get a Bite of The Feel Good Station "The Sound of Fiji". From the buzz on the streets to Fiji masti and mayhem to keep you entertained just the way you want!'[47]. There were several religious radio stations, some very recent and mostly with limited local reach: the Seventh Day Adventist 'Hope' station, with bible texts sent to mobile phones and a strong women's group noted for their music, and 'Harvest Radio FM97' or the 'Sounds of heaven' (part of 'Trinity Broadcasting Network' (TBN), World Harvest Broadcasting Network) with 'the very best in

---

[47]http://radiotime.com/station/s_101958/Bula_Namaste_F M_994.aspx/.

Christian music, plus anointed teaching and preaching from around the world, as well as local ministry from across the Body of Christ in Fiji'[48].

With this multiplicity of outlets, there seemed less need for the arguments prevalent in the 1970s about which genres of music should be broadcast popular music? jazz? Indian (or western) high-art music?) or the desirable balance between local and visiting artists: there were enough outlets to cover all. Rather it was a matter of competition between the many radio stations with their often overlapping musical offerings as they jostled for attention on the airways. Even FBCL, with all its advantages in government backing, overall reach and library resources, felt threatened by the competition. The VitiFM station on Communications Fiji Ltd for example put on the same kinds of songs to a similar Fijian target audience as FBCL's Bula FM so, as the FBLC's Director of music put it, the on-air announcers were constantly being reminded 'that they have to be lively and creative in their presentation so that they don't lose their listeners'[49].

48

http://cmfinternational.org.fj/index.php?option=com_conte
nt&task=view&id=19&Itemid=50/.
[49] Asaeli Ratuwara director of music FBCL email 1/5/09.

Radio was everywhere listened to and had a pervasive influence in both reflecting and shaping people's musical tastes. Decisions makers on the music to be broadcast – like Jokatama Qio - helped to structure not just people's listening but their perceptions. But FBCL radio no longer had the same direct patronage position as in the 1970s. Though there had in recent years been some field forays these were now less frequent than earlier both because of financial pressures and the already well-stocked musical archive. Its facilities were by now run down – as the FBCL Chief Executive put it they were 'state of the art – *1950s* state of the art!' –and it was no longer the main recording site for group playing. More important, the proliferation of multiple local recording studios - often better equipped, - meant that prospective groups for broadcasting regularly brought their locally recorded discs to the radio station rather than aiming for live performance and recording in its studios.

This was not to say that radio had ceased all support and incentive for local music: far from it. It was still the medium that both musicians and local music shops lobbied for broadcast attention and publicity. And though the 1970s style recordings were less frequent, they still sometimes happened in the FBCL studios and occasional field forays. An important intervention was in their frequent support for competitions, whether by direct sponsorship or by transmitting performances from events organised by others. Thus in April 2009 FBCL-organised a *bhajan* competition performed to a packed audience [50]. Events like the annual Hibiscus Festival, brimming with local musics and dance, were regularly transmitted over the radio, which sometimes itself sponsored particular items and competitions within it. Radio Fiji was the organiser for the 'Concert of Hope' held in the Albert Park to raise funds following disastrous Fiji floods early in 2009, with performances by 'some of Fiji's best bands and singers', among them groups like Jeriko, Divine, Bad Boys East,Carpe Diem, Cagi Mudre ni Delairoro, Eagles Wings, Malumu ni tobu ke Navaukura, First Tribe and Dokidoki and One2Eight .. [and] vocalists Seru Serevi, Ofa Ali, Ronald Jai, Jet Shiri Krishna, Sekove Raikoro and Peni Seniyasi.

Dance groups appeared too, as did the RFMF Military Band and the by-now legendary guitarist Tom Mawi just recovered from a serious illness

---

[50] FBCL website (http://www.radiofiji.com.fj/index.php) April 26 2009.

[51]. Not just for music bought in from elsewhere but for local productions across a wide span of genres, radio continued – if in a somewhat changing context - to be a crucial and active medium for locally performed music.

Radio had the further attraction, moreover, as a medium with which listeners could now interact on a personal basis. Just about all the radio stations had their own web presence through which it was possible to see personal profiles of the presenters and in some cases communicate with them direct through 'chat lines' where listeners not only in Fiji but around the world could talk live with announcers while on air. At FBCL, musicians and publicists sometimes dropped in in person to publicise their wares.

More important still – in fact crucial to the music being played – was the heavy use of listeners' requests. These 'dedications' were the basis of a substantial proportion of the output on most stations. Among the radio announcers' key tasks was responding to their listeners' wishes with the necessary material – easier for FBCL with its large music archive than for other stations, especially with the older numbers – and

---

[51] *Fiji Times* Jan 21, 2009 on-line
http://www.fijitimes.com/story.aspx?id=11233/.

presenting them on air with names and messages. Requests came in constantly.

For local listeners this was most often by phone or text message. Vodafone, the monopoly mobile provider in Fiji, set up daily competitions to encourage text messaging and this had become a popular channel of communication – one way in which radio stations aimed to engage their listeners. On those stations with a chat line system listeners could also make requests directly on-air. Fax was used too, so was email – a common route for those with computer access, with a pre-set slot on many websites making this easy. People were continually making contact to ask for a dedication, usually, as a Radio Fiji Gold announcer summed it up,

> a song played for the caller who calls in and dedicate songs to his/her families, friends, workmates, father, mother sister brother whether you're in hospital, prisons, on the seas in Fiji or overseas, rugby team, netball team etc if you have a dog we can also dedicate a song to the dog or cats (Sevanaia Tora.email 30/4/09).

A striking aspect of such requests - and the first of two general points to make about this 'moment' of 2009 - was how many requests came from overseas. Music and performers from Fiji

155

were hugely popular with Fijians abroad. FBCL's live radio streaming on the web (predominantly music) was attracting 26,000 visitors a month in 2009, over 75% from the US, New Zealand and Australia. The international listenership had become substantial, raising the profile of Fijian music and its local artists. The popularity of Fijian music – and to an extent Pacific music generally – was also forwarded by the spin-off from tourist enthusiasm: take-home discs sold extensively at the international airport. It was also spread through Fijian performers making international careers, outside as well as within Fiji, and their recorded discs – well publicised on the web – had become yet another source for requests to local radio back home.

The context for this international interest in requests for Fijian music lay particularly in the numbers of Fijians living abroad for whom Fiji was where their hearts still lay. Passionate requests came even from those who while in Fiji itself might have showed little interest in music. Once abroad 'some of them are even desperate and ask us if we can send the songs over to them, which we obviously can't because of copyright issues' (Soneel Ram 2Day FM email 15/4/09). Similarly on the Fijian-language music station Bula FM

We do get calls from the US, Australia, NZ, France from the rugby boys in Europe and of course Germany. Most of the callers are soldiers or students and others ... most of the dedications are for Fijians who are serving in the Middle East and those who have joined the British Army (Jokatama Qio, email 11/4/09).

Whether from indigenous Fijians, Indo-Fijians, or so-called Europeans and part-Europeans the radio and television stations were bombarded with messages requesting broadcast music from their homeland.

Some of those living abroad were native Fijians, sometimes only temporarily overseas as students or soldiers, but still keeping strong links with home. Fijian music was often heard throughout the house, and all over the world could be found Fijians sitting around (some kind of) 'grog' replacing the native kava to play and listen to music. There were numerous Fijian churches in California, New Zealand and Australia with services conducted in Fijian, doubtless with their Fijian hymn-singing; Fijian music was also in demand among Fijian regiments with the British Army in Germany where the local night clubs opted to play Fijian music.

The development of the internet had also made listening to Fijian music ever more possible throughout the world. Overseas Fijians created their own on-line communities [52] and sometimes ran their own radio programmes. Marketing of Fijian recordings discs was carried out on the web, sometimes with personal comments and interactions in both English and Fijian from Fijians abroad. On YouTube Daniel Rae Costello's videoed song 'We were Fiji' attracted a series of comments like 'O I luv you fiji. See you in March. And yes proud to be a fijian', 'I miss home', and 'Hey I love this song! Remind me of the days at USP [University of the South Pacific in Suva]! Love you Suva! Thanks for sharing!' ([53]). Added to this were the opportunities for down-loadable recordings from the Internet and live-streaming from FBCL and other radio stations. The transnational appreciation of Fijian music was notable indeed.

---

[52] e.g. http://www.ozfiji.com/#/, http://www.aucklandfiji.org.nz/, http://www.canterburypasifika.org.nz/fiji/?q=node/614/.
[53] YouTube comments on Daniel Rae Costello's videoed song 'We were Fiji' (http://www.youtube.com/watch?v=TMr3S4OiB E).

Fijians abroad – native Fijians that is – were important enough to the twenty-first practice if music. But they were dwarfed by the substantial numbers of Indo-Fijians who had emigrated.

There had long been a pattern of Indians moving overseas from Fiji. The multiple coups since 1987 had hugely increased this, not least the violence against Indo-Fijians in 2000 and their uncertainty about any future for them in Fiji itself. There had in consequence been a heavy exodus from Fiji to overseas countries such as New Zealand, Australia, Canada and west-coast USA. From the near equal population of Fijians and Indians in 1978 their numbers had dropped to an (estimated) 35% or so– an exodus of tens of thousands, no small proportion in an overall population of about 800,000. By 2009 , it was claimed, nearly one third of Indo-Fijians were living outside Fiji [54].

Here was a second Indian diaspora. And these 'twice-migrants' now looked not to India but to Fiji as their home. As Marshud Ali had put it, for them Fiji was 'the golden place'. It was a common theme. Despite the pain, 'in their heart

---

[54] Indigenous Fijians made up 57% of the total population of around 840,000 (Radio New Zealand 31.5.09).

Fiji was still magnetic'. An Auckland businessman who migrated to New Zealand after the 1987 coup admitted that 'in my conscience when the term "home" was used, what comes to mind was Fiji, not India', while for a 21-year-old physiotherapist who spent her first ten years in Fiji but now lived in New Zealand:

> My race was Indian but I'm a third generation Fijian ... Fiji was a part of me and my family members were raised there, lived there, we earned and lived off the land and gave back to it. After three generations we consider ourselves part of the land. Fiji was happiness, my childhood, safety, simplicity, beauty, sunsets that painted the sky crimson red, feeling of belonging, looking at a Fijian and seeing myself in them (Field 2006).

The Indo-Fijian communities abroad retained close connections both with each other and with their homeland. It was commonly held that just about every Indo-Fijian family in Fiji had at least one relation overseas, and there was constant coming and going as migrants kept up ties not just to Fiji as a whole but also, as with native Fijians, to particular locations within it. All the devices of modern communication technologies were being brought into play too: telephones, email, manifold ingenious interactions through the web, the marketing and circulation of CDs, DVDs, written texts and much else. Fijian-Hindi recordings were featured and discussed on the web. The Bhojpuri melodies that had been such a hit in Fiji in 2006 had circulated rapidly throughout the Fiji-Indian diaspora through durable and inexpensive digital video compact discs (VCDs) with their ease of duplication and dissemination ' the ideal qualities', as Miller puts it, 'for transnational media' (Miller 2008: 415).

Dedications of songs on local radio also played a significant part. It meant something to be in touch with radio announcers operating direct from Fiji itself, hear music from their home and make a connection with their families and friends in Fiji. Thus dedications for the most recent songs came in to Radio Mirchi – the Hindi youth station - not just from Australia and New Zealand, but from even more scattered Indo-Fijians in China and Trinidad, keeping the radio staff on their toes.

This new diaspora was relevant for migrating musics. No longer just a 19th and 20th century diasporic culture with imaginations drawn to an Indian homeland these contemporary 'twice-migrants' looked to their roots in Fiji. Transnational indeed in this new diaspora India was the first origin; but Fiji, with its beauty and its music and its land which they themselves had helped to create, was now the homeland with which their hearts were entwined.

The second striking characteristic of the 2009 (and continuing) music scene in and around Fiji was that in the midst of both the creative innovations in music-making and the many transnational links there was at the same time a stress on 'our' tradition and the 'authentic' ways of the past. This was evident, if in differing contexts, among both Fijians and Indians. It was perhaps not surprising among migrants or temporary sojourners away from home. As Fernando Lobendahn of FijiTV commented, even those little involved in Fijian music while in Fiji 'loved the sounds of it when they all migrated ... it could also mean that they were all homesick' (email xx/04/09). But, interestingly, it seemed to be one facet even in some of the 'local' musics among those staying in Fiji.

What was felt as the 'authentic' and 'ancestral' tradition varied with both genre and timescale. As elsewhere it was a matter of perception and construction rather than the outcome of unchanging historical continuity.

For native Fijians, hymn singing was unquestionably part of their habitual way of life, deeply engrained in the Fijian consciousness and manifested in the repeated cycles of the religious year. Hymns might be sung with new rhythms and at times words, but the practice of hymn-singing had entered into the Fijian self-image contrasted to the undisciplined (or so it was seen) noise of street music, American pop, or non-Christian Indian intruders. Quintessential Fijian identity was from one perspective seen to coincide with Christianity – just about all native Fijians were Christian – above all the Methodist church as the somehow 'natural' religion of the land, counterposed to Indians with their foreign incoming religions. [55] Whether Methodist or not, hymns were known to the majority of indigenous Fijians (Tuquota 2006: 64). Here was the authentic interaction with the abiding Christian God and his voices on earth, figuring large in the projection of Fiji's image in discs on sale abroad and in the duty free shops of Fiji's international airport. 'There was no doubt', in Finau Hu'akau Tuquota's assessment, that 'hymn singing had united the indigenous Fijian people' (Tuquota 2006: 64).

There was something about guitars too. Not a predominant part of the scene in, say, 1937,

---

[55] Even those Indians (a very small proportion) who were Christians were sometimes seen by native Fijians to have imported foreign Hindu ways in to the church, and in the main worshipped separately.

guitars – so long as they were acoustic - were now regarded as typically part of Fijian musical tradition, something to be harked back to and, together with ukuleles, to be encouraged amidst the surfeit of amplified instrumentation. People met to sing to a guitar round the bowl of yaqona, a valued part of shared Fijian tradition with its associated ceremony, and many of the Fijian local groups used acoustic guitars in their line-up. The 2008 meke competition that had attracted so much interest throughout Fiji was specifically designed as 'traditional Fijian music', specifying only acoustic guitars (Apakuki Waqa Fiji Radio 1). The same to an extent went for the quieter melodic harmonising sometimes projected as typical of Pacific music. The FBCL music library till recently provided the 'Boarding Music' for the Fiji carrier Air Pacific and a notice was still pinned up there about what was required: no 'metal-based, heavy beat, falsetto and energetic' music, but 'tasteful and soothing' music, with instrumentals and songs 'based on Fijian rhythms'.

But it was still the *meke* that was seen as *the* traditional Fijian form. Indeed this high-culture and (consequentially perhaps) conservative form was probably the most resistant to change of all the Fijian genres. Going beyond that, there was a special aura about something performed under that name. Even newly composed *mekes* or ones where performers used what might be regarded as newer rhythms, instruments or words, the form still had about it a whiff of the authentic tradition. Its mysterious and 'centuries-old' quality was highlighted for the tourist market too, pictured amidst swaying palms, ocean on the beach and inspiration from the old gods and spirits: here, it was claimed under a heading of 'Chanting island style', was 'the real traditional Fijian music' [56]).

It was not just in tourist contexts either. It was widely praised, and the only musical form mentioned – as 'an ongoing tradition' - on the 2009 official government site about 'Fijian culture and tradition' [57]. Local participants articulated a similar ideology, even where the particular cases scarcely fully accorded with the rhetoric of an inspired traditional vehicle from the past or of a historic instrumentation restricted to clapping, lali drum and bamboo strikers.

The *meke* tradition was also validated, and crucially so, through its association with chiefshipmand ancestral tradition, a part of Fijian heritage therefore that was to be accorded recognition even by those whose personal

---

[56] ('Chanting island style',
http://www.fijilive.com/fijimagic/view.php?mlx=11&st=73&frm=chanting%20island%20style consulted 21/05/09/.
[57] http://www.fiji.gov.fj/publish/history_culture.shtml/.

preferences might lie with other musical genres. This was the form, it was held, in which history was passed down, in the unwritten 'songs of our forefathers' (Miri): 'Europeans write it down with paper and pen, we write it down on *meke'* said Tuilevu Vosa, himself a composer. Just as artists overseas *write* their compositions, explained one (very literate) Fijian, here 'it is in our blood' to create and perform *mekes*.

In the performance and witnessing of *meke*, with its beautiful dance gestures as well as singing and traditional percussion, ideally in the full wonderful *meke* dress with leaves, flowers and bodies gleaming with oil, Fijians expressed and celebrated a salient symbol of their 'true' Fijian tradition and identity, that image well honed in the tourist industry but also consonant with what was seen as a long Fijian tradition.

This was so whether resident inside or outside Fiji. *Meke* performers travelled to represent Fiji in competitions abroad (they were famed winners of several in Hong Kong in the 1990s), Fijian migrants in America, New Zealand and Australia requested them on the radio and, so the rhetoric went, passed them on to their children: they 'will never disappear'. As a local Fijian scholar summed it up, it had become 'the traditional Fijian link that binds the Fijians, *vanua* and its culture together', *vanua* being the whole Fijian world, physical, human and spiritual (Tuqota 2006: 40).

Among Indo-Fijians it worked differently. For them there was little overt tourist motivation – Indian culture had no mention on official tourist sites, was relatively seldom highlighted in tourist resorts, and did not figure in the airport souvenir shops. But another discourse around authenticity was noticeable.

As Kevin Christopher Miller demonstrated so clearly in his thesis 'A community of sentiment: Indo-Fijian music and identity discourse in Fiji and its diaspora' (2008) it took several directions.

One was the authenticity still attached to the cycle of the Hindu and Muslim years and the music associated with them, continuing through the years of indenture and connecting Indo-Fijians into that shared past. The detailed performance manifestations might – like Fijian *mekes* - have changed over the years and the interpretation of 'the tradition' be related to the particular experiences and actions of Indians as they lived in Fiji, but the discourse connecting the devotional song tradition and the songs associated with festivals such as *Holi* laid heavy emphasis on the authenticity of these musical forms. *Ramayana* recitations and *Ramlila* dramas with their musical manifestations were deeply bound into family, religious and cultural heritage, connecting their participants directly with the Indo-Fijian indenture past. It also, if more remotely, linked to the ancient culture of India whose classical music attracted respect as a symbol of an authentic great tradition, together with the bhajans and religious song genres recognised in both India (sometimes South Asia more widely) and in Fiji. The more ancient high-art music had its admirers in Fiji – more so probably than in 1978 – and as perhaps with all classical forms carried a validating mark of antiquity. But for most Indo-Fijans whether in Fiji or abroad it was primarily an authenticity from music that could be associated with their shared indenture heritage. This came through for example in the faag songs performed at the Holi festival. New songs were composed locally but the genre and its re-creation were experienced as an unbroken tradition from the agricultural days of the indentured labourers in Fiji (Miller 2008: 221-3).

Also important as authenticating a sense of belonging, was the Bollywood music – transnational but also a part of local Fiji experience. Clearly more 'modern' than the *Ramayana* text but in some ways growing out of it, Hindi cinema had enormous popularity among Indo-Fijians in both Fiji and abroad. It carried an immediacy and meaningful frame of reference, a link held in common among Indo-Fijians and drawing them together in shared imaginative experience. As Manas Ray reported of Indo-Fijians now in Australia but recalling their upbringing in Fiji

> Bollywood created its own public and psychic platform for people to interact. (My numerous respondents have narrated how as boys or girls, they used to gather around the movie halls long before show-time). The gossip columns, the 24-hour Hindi service, the occasional visits of singers and stars from the then Bombay – all this went into constituting the culture of a community which harboured no illusion of return [to India] but for reasons of identity and cultural make-up, yearned for a romanticised version of India that Bollywood amply provided. The genealogy of unprecedented popularity of the mass cultural tradition of Bollywood in Fiji thus lies in the diasporic re-discovery of 'little' traditions that the *girmitiyas* [indentured labourers] brought with them and preserved over a century (Ray 2004: 257)

The mass images of India transmuted through Hindi film and its romantically suffused music gave a broad symbolic frame for a fantasy of both shared roots and a vision of the modern world today to which they were linked, a mark of cultural identity. As Miller put it, Indo-Fijians continued to draw on 'aesthetics and ideologies associated with a modern but imagined India' (Miller 2006: xviii). The discourse surrounding these various Indo-Fijian musics was brought to bear even when the music itself might well in fact be a mix of style from varying sources. Bollywood had of course long drawn on elements of western popular music as well as Indian folk and classical music together with mutual influences with devotional religious singing; and recently there had been further influences from rap and Latin American music. But it still in a sense encapsulated a link to the dream of timeless yet modern India. In practice, as Manas Ray explains, Fiji-Indian young people were using such re-mixes 'to fashion a discourse of authenticity' (2006: 266).

The active association between music and religion as a symbol of identity was perhaps even more meaningful among the 'twice migrants', the second Indo-Fijian diasporas where migrants tended to congregate in large numbers, forge strong community ties, and set up their own associations [58].Whether in California, Canada, or

---

[58] e.g. the (Indo-Fijian) Fiji Association in Auckland New Zealand, first founded in 1977, was in 2009 sponsoring cultural delegations to New Zealand from both Fiji and India, including dancers and musicians chosen for their

170

New Zealand Fijian Indians launched celebrations reminiscent of the practices in Fiji - for Fiji Independence Day, *Holi, Diwali*. They held *Ramayana* recitals, staged competitions of Fiji-style *qawali* and *bhajan* singing, and listened on the web to music on the Hindi programmes of radio from Fiji (Miller 2008: 390, 384). Among Indo-Fijians in Australia *Ramayana* recitals, *Ramlila* dramas and *bhajan* singing were perhaps even more popular than in Fiji itself. Hindi films too, with their potent mythification of India, the once-mother, were central to a whole range of local activities, above all among the young. In the Indo-Fijian suburbs in Sydney, as Ray points out, this came in a range of media - 'bands specialising in Hindi film music, music schools for filmy songs, DJs, karaoke singers, film magazines and community radio programmes' (Ray 2004: 259).)

The diasporic discourse was a complex one. Some link to India was recognised, as was the cultural relationship to certain Indian musical genres, and artists and musical recordings from India were welcome among Indo-Fijians abroad as they were in Fiji. But the link was in some ways a tenuous one. At the centre lay the musical experience of Fiji and an assertion of the Fijian-

---

excellence in sarod, sitar and other classical Indian music.(http://www.fijiassociation.co.nz/AboutUs.html/.

Indian experience and way of doing things. The particular soundscape of Fijian-style Ramayana mandali with their familiar Fijian repertoire of songs, and of tambura bhajan singing still rang in people's ears. The Ramayana recitals, faag singing, the make-up of Indo-Fijian instrumental ensembles, and melodies and performance styles attributed to the indenture period (Miller 2008: 428) marked a continuity, it was felt, with the indenture experience in Fiji – an experience not shared with Indians of *non*-Fijian roots. As one Indo-Fijian now in Auckland differentiated the Indo-Fijian practice from that of *Indian* Indians

> The tambura bhajan is not known to [subcontinental] Indians. And when they recite Ramayan, they only sing the main parts. In our Fijian way of doing it we sing all the lyrics and the pracharak will stop and explain. The idea is to get people involved in singing. I suppose that keeping that alive is the only way we can say that we're Fijians (quoted in Miller 2008: 406).

It was their *Fijian*-Indian cultural allegiance that was being enacted through their music. India was something other, no longer where they belonged or the land to which they owed allegiance. India might be the ancient origin, but in music as in their deeper emotions, Fiji was the true home.

These variegated discourses of 'authenticity' in many ways ran counter to, or at any rate co-existed with, both the facts of changing and blending musics, and of individuals' interest in innovation and experiment, something evident among musicians and listeners in both Fiji and its diasporic migrants. They might also seem to sit somewhat uneasily with the many ways that over the years individuals and groups had manipulated the musical resources at their disposal in new combinations, and the many changes in musical fashions, media settings and social conditions evident between 1937, 1978 and 2009, not to speak of all the years before and since those dates.

There were disputes too between different sections and localities as to which of their competing forms were the truly 'traditional' ones. But people through the ages have after all from time to time, wished to call on what at any given time they see as their 'tradition' or the 'true' ways which they wish to emphasise in particular settings. Music, powerful symbol as well as deep dimension of human experience, is indeed a potent locale for such a framework, both as articulated discourse and felt reality.

And it was not just a matter of rhetoric. To those involved the musical re-enactments of the *Ramayana* text, of Methodist hymns, Handel's

Messiah, the music-dance-costume of the *meke*, Gilbert and Sullivan arias, even, for later generations, the Beatles, a golden Bollywood melody or the lovely Fiji farewell song *isa lei* carried a link to a repertoire which in some sense was deeply-rooted as their own. To the participants, as to others engaged in musics in many other places, these intimations of somehow timeless authenticity, coming from different directions as they did for native Fijians and for Fijian Indians and in contrasting political circumstances was not the only aspect of their music but did indeed in some contexts represent a deeply resonant dimension of their musical activities.

PART 4 MUSIC AND MUSICS

Chapter 12   So what travels, and how?

So – for music, what travels and how does it cone about?

It might seem that, from the known theoretical frameworks and accounts if other places we already have the answer. But as far as Fiji goes one commonly offered answer that does *not* fit the bill is the often-told story of western musics sweeping out onto the far-off lands islands and taking over there, whether through the imperial expansion of earlier years or, nowadays, through the apparently all-enveloping mass media propulsion of Euro-American pop.

It is of course no new idea that the ethnocentric story of western success in taming and civilising the globe with its culture is no longer acceptable. But it is surprising how deeply it has influenced our perceptions. Yes indeed there has been mutual contact between Fijians and many western nations - but also with Tongans, with other Pacific Islanders, with Australians, Indians, and South Asia generally. Fiji was no untouched Pacific paradise of aboriginal natives, some 'other' essentially contrasted to 'the west', into which a western content could be poured.

Nor can Fiji's changing musics with all their complexities be shovelled into universal global epochs, whether these are defined in terms of the British colonial project (pre-colonial, colonial, post-colonial) or - in another seductive image - of overwhelming technological waves pushing all before them. The media did indeed have their importance for migrating music. But their interactions played out in more complex ways than allowed in the western-oriented vision of a foreordained upward curve of oral to literate to electronic or – in alternative metaphor – of tradition to modernity. Music and its changes in Fiji, as elsewhere, are notably more complex than can possibly be allowed for in that large story of irresistible western expansion.

But perhaps the answer to 'what travels?!' is not 'music' either or even (my preferred term here) 'musics' themselves. Music, like language, is intertwined deep in human consciousness and action, of the body and the emotions not just our cognition. When we travel we bring our soundscapes and our conventions for speech and song with us and interact with new conventions we encounter along the way.

I do not think it is best to think of this process as *music* travelling – any more than we speak of 'language migrating'. Rather, as will doubtless

have emerged throughout my account, I prefer to see it as a matter
people actively engaging, in a whole variety of both old and new ways, in a range of musical practices feeding on influences from many cultures.

The concepts of 'globalisation', 'the diaspora culture', ' the global and the local' and 'hybridity' have been used to describe such interactions. Neither they nor similar abstract terms seem to me to throw much but a fairly superficial light on the actual processes. Worse, they have too often served as an alibi for avoiding the harder travail of actually digging into the facts: of what people actually *do*, when, how, where, and when.

Something the same could be said of the commonly used term 'world music'. This at first sight looks precise and useful. But, as well explained in Toynbee.) it is often not realised that the term was created *not* as a label for an already delimited category but as a gather-all word for all those discs that book shops didn't know where to shelve or on-line sellers to classify. It was a marketing tool, plain and simple. Translation: miscellaneous; the rest; the others, things outside the mainstream of properly recognised music; the hodge podge the bits we don't know where to put.

My own treatment of local music in an English town (1989) is classified as 'classic music' and similar categories on the English Amazon website but in amazon.com (for the U.S.) in the 'world music. category. This for *English* music! But no more inappropriate than to dub Fijian music-making and recordings as 'world music'.

All music and music-making are after all locally practised together with strands of international influences that are being locally realised - the musicians making them their own - from the world. Classing this as some unknown othering entity is nit so unlike the once popular 'primitive' or 'developing' categorisations or even - while useful when used non- judgementally - the potentially marginalising term of 'ethnomusicology'

It is of course right to acknowledge the swathes of influence and mutual interactions that throughout history have spread around the world, musical, political, economic, cultural, affecting local practices - and not just from the west. These are the settings in which people act. But it is *people* who operate and build shared experiences, whether innovative or conventional or, perhaps inescapably, a mixture of the two. They work with the musical resources to hand, wherever these may have come from.

So whether in the past from north Indian folk genres, contending tradition or Hindu musical recitation, Tongan dance or English brass band playing, from jazz or rock, or more recently from hip hop, so-called 'world music' or the latest Bollywood hits - from all these diverse and themselves mixed musical forms and more people have selected and rejected, and in both listening and playing turned things to their own tastes.

In thinking about musics it is too simple to analyse the process by which they apparently move primarily in terms of transmission in 'bottled' media across time and space. That may indeed be part of the picture, and interestingly. But without also attending to those who now or in the past have realised and enacted musics in new and in old settings we miss the full picture. In Fiji as elsewhere, musical genres, ideologies, instruments, conventions were available at many periods and from many origins not as some automatic presence but as resources to draw on and manipulate – it was human beings who did so and made their choices.

Writing in another context, Bruce Johnson makes the point well.

The global production industry is not the centre of gravity of music in and of a community. Of course it gives us tools which we customise, restructure and whose meanings we make over. But apart from these acts of appropriation we also make our own music out of local materials (Johnson 2008: 86).

His words could equally be applied to Fiji and to the musical traditions of the South Pacific - or anywhere.

Of course people's actions in making musics travel – or, as I would put it, engaging in both continuing and changing musical conventions in new settings – did not take place in a vacuum. Some people and groups have always had greater influence than others, and in Fiji as elsewhere music was enacted within the complex specificities of particular historical contexts where not all was consensus or simple continuity. The framework of religion was one powerful if variegated context for much music-making in Fiji amidst its local as well as international links – with multiple internal variations and changes certainly but remarkably persistent. Important too were the varying ideologies surrounding music and its diverse practices and the settings in which they operated, permeated by the outlooks and politics of their day. There was the colonial Fiji of 1937 with its still fairly recent history of indentured labour contrasting with the 1978 independent nation or, later, with the post-coups military control of 2009, with the continuing themes of (native) Fijian political power and of constructed political-racial labelling with their implications for music – conditions which help to illuminate the emphasis at certain periods of variously constructed concepts of authenticity amidst homesickness, perceived threats or assertions of authority.

People also act, everywhere, using the media resources of their time, all – even in the 1930s – unquestionably offering opportunities for musics to travel: that is, to be carried, whether unconsciously or deliberately by people moving from place to place: tunes, rhythms, religious and social rituals, lullabies, instruments, texts ... . So the changing media conditions between our three moments were also significant.

Live performance was always one medium, enacted within the conventional genres, innovations and, without doubt, disagreements of the time and carried in people's bodies and memories as they both travelled and stayed put. But then – at varying times – there were also the devices through which music could be 'bottled'. Only in the last couple of centuries has it been feasible to capture sound so as to be heard at a different time or a different place and by a different audience from those of its live performance.

By 1937 music could indeed be caught so as to a degree transcend time and space. There were the largely one-way media of that earlier moment, especially vinyl recordings and radio plus (just starting) film, together with the fixing of certain (limited) elements of music in hard copy text – all effective and well-known media by then though not all easily available to everyone or with much local input. Different in 1978 was the range of much more widely available media from both local and international sources, the locally controlled presence of recorded music in a variety of cheaper and more accessible forms - media furthermore that could be manipulated by both individuals and groups for their diverse musical purposes.

By 2009 the media were yet more interactive, not least for their digital basis, coming in multiple forms that enabled not just greater individual control and local experimentation but rapid and inexpensive multi-media musical exchange and mutual influences across transnational networks.

In radio in particular – that continuous, if changing, thread in music action - there had been the striking change in Fiji from the 1937 scenario almost wholly shaped by *in*coming transmissions and transcriptions from overseas – from Britain, from Australia, from India – to the fully fledged local radio of 1978 with its own voice, then on to the multiple radio channels of

2009 that also spoke *outwards* to the world from Fiji: its many local channels listened to in Fiji indeed but also called on by Fijian listeners from throughout the world and heard over the web in both hemispheres and a dozen countries.

'Travelling' music then.... We come back to the people. I have only been able to point to a small handful among myriads: those who not only, we presume, in various ways delighted in music but must also have *worked,* travailed, that it might survive, and might continue to sing for the following generations and after. In the South Pacific −or anywhere - *musics* did not if itself travel − fly forth like birds over the ocean - but lived and changed in and through the actions of many thousands of individuals and groups.

So we have to remember these many active practitioners. There were those who travelled the seas or the airways as migrants with their memories and music; the native Tongan missionaries who away back brought 'the message of God's love' − and the Methodist hymns - to Fiji; the conductors and members of church choirs or the *Ramayana mandali* singers over the years; the unpretentious taxi-driver, just one of the many thousands of participants in Fijian-style Hindu devotional songs; Krishna Murti and his band using guitars in new ways; creators of Fijian rap songs; professional Fijian

183

singers like Daniel Rae Costello or George 'Fiji' Veikoso using old and new motifs to shape new styles in Fiji and abroad; callers to Fiji's radio to request songs and the local hosts like Jokatama Qio who shaped the local radio programmes heard both within Fiji and abroad, presenters and librarians who found – or perhaps don't find – the required songs, self-taught musicians as singers, instrumentalists, band members; the field recorders and bands who recorded the audio-cassettes and discs in radio archive or marketing web sites, composers of faag songs or of mekes, and experimenters with Fijian rap songs or new ways with Bollywood tunes; those who in music wish at any one point to highlight what they see as the 'traditional'; the many names of musicians and listeners I have mentioned in passing during this paper; – even in his way Beresford Clark with his listening to Gilbert and Sullivan in the Suva of 1937 and his long encouragement for the local radio, that continuing resource for Fiji's musicians through those moments and locations – and more.

Chapter 13 Conclusion: from thence and hither to here and hence

Three 'moments' have been the occasion to explore, however sketchily, something of the complexities of music and its national, regional and international setting in the island nation of Fiji in the South Pacific. Fiji may be small. But in its history and presence it illustrates one crucial dimension of the travels and travails of music: that it is people who create music: those who practise music in some way ,by their composing, discussing, battling (it is worth it!), playing, listening, *using*. It is this that the history of Fiji's music reveals, vastly more illuminating than the abstractions about its nature or travels, however grand or initially convincing they may sound, far less than those hypothetical abstractions set up in ethnocentric west-centred paradigms.

In the context of Fiji and its environs we have seen music-making and its conceptualisation move from a point where to many – but emphatically not to all – culture and more particularly music was owned by and emanated from Britain (above all London), sent out from there – thence - to the ever-benighted or the, unfortunately, exiled-from-Britain peoples in 'the rest' of the world, transmitted under the kind auspices of British imperial rule and the BBC's Empire Service.

Then came the situation of increasingly-heard local radio, locally recorded musical resources, local musical groups forcing recognition, expanding international links. 'Here', Fiji and the South Pacific, is now somewhere.

Finally we come to the moment when it is now a matter of 'thence' as well as (as in every other country of the world)'hither'. Now we see Fiji and its musicians and radio operators in the world, calling and responding to its home dwellers and its diasporic, followers throughout the world.

What the future will bring, who can tell? There are many 'moments' still to come. But we may be sure that whatever the events, happy or cataclysmic as they befall, the practice of music, as in even the direst settings of the past, will continue, and continue, as its practitioners carry us forward, to inspire and soften the world.

I have not yet contacted Fiji radio to request a music dedication for myself (though I have once, and most touchingly, had one requested for me). But I know that, from here in England, no -Fijian as I am, I always can Perhaps when I have finished this I will do so. So close have we been brought across the Pacific, across the world, by the practitioners of music.

APPENDICES

Appendix 1 Note on sources

The account in this book is based on a mix of documentary and field sources. The latter were collected through participant observation during my stay in Fiji 1975-8, in the final months of which I undertook an intensive study of urban musics and musicians in the capital town Suva, based mainly on informal interviews, wider contacts and observation. This was supplemented by local documentary sources and a short research   visit to Suva in April 2009, using, again,   participant   observation,   informal interviews (sometimes with email follow-ups), research in the extensive South Pacific collection in the University of the South Pacific's Library, and the truly astounding music library of Indian, European, native Fijian , and other local musics held by Radio Fiji.

For the earlier period I was immensely helped by the rich resources of the known   BBC Radio Archive in Reading, England, on which the 1937 account is heavily dependent, supplemented by other published and unpublished material in a variety if archives and libraries in Fiji, Auckland and London. There was, and is, also a wealth of material in the web, and the resources, both audio and video in Fiji's now plentiful radio stations.

There is by now a large secondary literature on Fiji which I have also drawn on extensively, some of it unpublished (I would note especially the valuable dissertations Tuqota 2006 and Miller 2008). Many of these provided essential background information and contexting though none addressed precisely the issues treated here. The nearest were Tony Mitchell's *Popular music and local identity: Rock, pop and rap in Europe and Oceania* (1998) and Philip Hayward's *Sound alliances: indigenous peoples, popular music and cultural politics in the Pacific* (1998): both helpful but neither up to date on the local detail or, specially the first, theoretically illuminating, nor did either give a detailed account of Fiji, its complex music heritage(s) or its long and fascinating history). The general books on such subjects as globalisation, diaspora cultures, so-called 'world music', or popular music more generally, again sometimes provided useful insight but with the exceptions n of the excellent according Nat's in the multi-volume Grove series seldom had much substantial to say about South Pacific island cultures .

Abbreviations for sources used
Besides the conventional referencing forms I have used the following:

BBC WAC BBC   Written Archives, Reading,
,England.

A/2, B/2 ... for 1978 and 2009, references to
the placement in my manuscript notes.

Web references: given as consulted in 2014-15
(some may no longer be accessible)

Appendix 2. People: Notes on the main individuals mentioned

J. B. (later Sir (John) Beresford) Clark (1902–1968), Director of BBB Empire Service 1935-8, later posts included Controller of Overseas Services and Director of External Services (retired 1964)

Totaram Sanadhya (1876–1947), Indian indentured labourer in Fiji from 1893, later farmer, pundit, political activist, and follower of Gandhi after return to India in 1914

Ram Chandra Sharma, preacher and religious singer from India, in Fiji 1930-35

Olga Parshotam, Fellow of Trinity College of Music, music teacher in Suva in 1970s and 1980s

Tomasi (Tom) Mawi, leading jazz guitarist, Fiji, 1978 and later

Krishna Murti, Indo-Fijian guitarist, leader of 'Gurus' band, 1978

Yaminiasi Gaunavou, Fijian farmer and announcer at Fiji Broadcasting Commission, leader of 'Gaunavou' Fijian youth band 1978 (later eminent broadcaster and (Dec 2008) Chairman Fiji Broadcasting Corporation Ltd)

Marshud Ali, Indo-Fijian living near Suva, taxi-driver, 2009

Jokatama Qio, Fijian radio presenter for Bula FM, the vernacular (Fijian) pop station for Fiji Broadcasting Corporation Ltd 2009

Robin Palmer, English-born consulting engineer, conductor of Fiji Arts Club Choir since 1992

Daniel Rae Costello, Fiji-born singer, composer and sound engineer, creator of 'Aqualypso' style

George Veikoso (stage name 'Fiji') professional Fijian singer and composer, popular entertainer in Hawaii in 2009

Juniya Noah, native Fijian singer of Indian popular and religious music

Michelle Rounds, transnational jazz singer/songwriter of mixed Pacific heritage

Appendis 3 Glossary of Fijian and Indian musical terms used in the book

bhajan – devotional song, hymn (generic term) – Indo-Fijian.

bakhti – form of devotional Hinduism emphasising prayer and song, very popular in Fiji.

daunivucu – inspired *meke* composer (native Fijian).

dholak – double-headed Indian drum (membranophone).

filmi – songs from or in the style of Bollywood film (Indo-Fijian).

ghazal – song in Urdu, often light romantic (Indo-Fijian).

kirtan – responsorial chorus-leader devotional hymn (Indo-Fijian).

lali – native Fijian wooden slit drum (idiophone).

mandali – Fijian-Indian devotional singing group.

meke – native Fijian song-dance.

qawali – Indo-Fijian genre of solo singing to instrumental ensemble (as developed in Fiji this had little similarity to the original Sufi form).

Ramayana – sacred Indian text, central to Indo-Fijian music in its Tulsidas version.

tambura – Indo-Fijian single-string plucked lute, locally made.

yaqona (Fijian) kava, 'grog' – ritual /social (non-alcoholi drink..

Appendix *4. Radio services in Fiji 1937-2009*

1937 AWA (Amalgamated Wireless (Australasia) Ltd) through its local subsidiary Fiji Broadcasting Co. Ltd. With many retransmissions from the BBC in London.

1978 FBC Fiji Broadcasting Commission

2009 FBCL Fiji Broadcasting Corporation Ltd (part government sponsored, part commercial)

CFM Communications Fiji Ltd, independent South Pacific broadcasting company

Several smaller stations, religious and other

Select Bibliography

Barney, Ralph D. (1978) 'Pacific Islands', in Lent, John A. (ed.) *Broadcasting in Asia and the Pacific*, Philadelphia: Temple University Press.

Bohlman, Philip V. (2002) *World Music: A Very Short Introduction*, OXford: Oxford University Press.

Brenneis, Donald (1987) 'Performing passions: aesthetics and politics in an occasionally egalitarian community', *American Ethnologist* 14: 236-50.

Brenneis, Donald (1991) 'Aesthetics, performance, and the enactment of tradition in a Fiji Indian community', in Appadurai, A. et al. (eds) *Gender, genre, and power in South Asian expressive traditions*, Philadelphia: University of Pennsylvania Press.

Brenneis, Donald (1998) 'Musical migrations: Indians in Fiji', in Kaeppler and Love: 92-4.

Burton, J. W. and Deane, W. (1936) *A hundred years in Fiji*, London: Epworth Press.

Business, April 27 2006: *http://www.pacificislands.cc/pm82003/index.php* (http://archives.pireport.org/archive/2006/April/04-27-ft2.htm printout).

Cattermole, Jennifer (2007) ' "Fiji Blues?": Taveuni and Qamea Musicians'

Engagements with recording technologies' / ' « Blues des Fiji ?" : Les musiciens Taveuni et Qamea et l'engagement avec les technologies d'enregistrement', *World of music* 49, 1: 231 [?], 2 : 171-187.

Colonial Office (1936) *Interim report of a committee on broadcasting services in the colonies*, London: Colonial Office Misc, 469.

Coulter, John Wesley (1942) *Fiji. Little India of the Pacific*, Chicago: University of Chicago Press.

Collins, Ken G. (1967) *Broadcasting grave and gay*, Christ Church New Zealand: Caxton Press.

Derby, Mark and Wilson, Helen (1995) 'Pacific Islander radio and music in Auckland', *Perfect Beat* 2/2 1995.

Field, Michael (2006) 'Fiji's future uncertain as Indians continue exodus', *Islands*.

Fiji Government (1970) *The Report of the Broadcasting Review Committee 1969/70 together with A Report on the Fiji Radio Audience Survey June/Sept. 1969,* Suva: Government Printer.

Finnegan, Ruth (1979, 1981) 'Musical groups in Suva', *Fiji Heritage* Dec 1979: 1-7, Oct. 1981: 1-7.

Finnegan, Ruth (1992) *Oral poetry,* 2nd edition, Bloomington: Indiana University Press.

Finnegan, Ruth (1989) *The hidden musicians Music-making in an English town,*

Cambridge: Cambridge University Press (2nd edition Wesleyan University Press, 2007).

Finnegan, Ruth (2013) *Music and creation,* Bletchley: Callender Press.

Finnegan, Ruth (2015) *The height of music: essays in musical thought,* Bletchley: Callender Press.

Finnegan, Ruth and Pillai, Raymond (eds) (1978) *Essays on Pacific literature,* Oral Tradition Series, 2, Suva: Fiji Museum.

Glamuzina, Kaye (2001) 'Melanesia, Fiji', in Sadie, S (ed) *The New Grove Dictionary of Music and Musicians,* vol 16, London: Macmillan,

Goldsworthy, David (1998) 'Popular music: Fiji'; 'Fijian .music', in Kaeppler and Love: 161-2, 774-76.

Henderson, G. C. (1931) *Fiji and the Fijians 1835-1856,* Sydney: Angus and Robertson.

Johnson, Bruce (2008) Review of Finnegan 'Hidden Musicians', *Perfect Beat* 8, 4: 85-7.

Kaeppler, Adrienne L. and Love, J. W. (eds) (1998) *Australia and the Pacific (The Garland Encylopedia of World Music,* Vol. 9), New York: Garland Publishing Inc.

Kaisau, Semiti (1978) 'The functions of Fijian *mekes*', in Finnegan and Pillai.

Kelly, John D. (1988) 'From Holi to Diwali in Fiji: an essay on ritual and history', *Man* 23: 40-55.

Kelly, John D. and Kaplan, Martha (2001) *Represented communities. Fiji and world decolonization*, Chicago: University of Chicago Press.

Kubuabola, Solaila, Seniloli, Ama andVatucawaqa, Losana (1978) 'Poetry in Fiji: a general introduction', in Finnegan and Pillai.

Lal, Brij (ed.) (2004) *Bittersweet: the Indo-Fijian experience*, Canberra: Pandanus Books.

Lee, Dorothy Sara (1998) 'Fijian music', in Kaeppler and Love: 776ff.

Manuel, Peter (1991) *Popular Musics of the Non-Western World: An Introductory Survey*, New York: Oxford University Press.

Mayer, Adrian (1973 [1961]) *Peasants in the Pacific. A study of Fiji Indian rural society* 2nd edn, London: Routledge & Kegan Paul.

Miller, Kevin Christopher (2008) *A community of sentiment: Indo-Fijian music and identity discourse in Fiji and its diaspora*, doctoral thesis, University of California, Los Angeles.

Mitchell, Tony (2002) *Global noise. Rap and hip hop outside the USA*, Middletown: Wesleyan University Press..,

Nilan, Pam (2004/5) 'Popular music and dance in urban Fiji: a divided cultural landscape', *Perfect Beat* 7. 1/2 :??

'Plymouth Report' (1936) *see* Colonial Office 1936.

Power, D. S. (1995) *Diversity: the soul of public radio*, Wellington: Winston Churchill Memorial Trust Board.

Ramnarine, Tina Karina (1996) '"Indian " music in the diaspora: case studies of "chutney" in Trinidad and in London', *British Journal of Ethnomusicology* 5: 133-53.

Ravuvu, Asesela (1991) *The facade of democracy*, Suva: Reader Publishing House.

Ray, Manas (2006) 'Bollywood and diaspora: Fiji Indians, from indenture to globalisation', in Ghosh, Lipi and Chatterjee, Ramaksrishna (eds) (2006) *Indian diaspora in Asian and Pacific regions. Cultures, people, interactions*, Jaipur: Rawat Publications.

Roth, George Kingsley (ed.) (1937) *Fiji: Handbook of the colony 1938*, 4th edn, Suva: Acting Government Printer.

Sampson, Sam (1998) 'South-Sea-Island magic - Bill Sevesi and the Auckland Music Scene', *Perfect Beat* 4/1.

Sanadhya, Totaram (2003) *My twenty-one years in the Fiji Islands*, ed. and trans. (from the Hindi) by Kelly, J. D. and Singh, U. K., 2nd edition, Suva: Fiji Museum.

Saumaiwai, Chris (1977) '*Meke* wesi' [Record review] *Ethnomusicology* 21, 2 353-4.

Slobin Mark (ed.) (2008) *Global soundtracks,* Middletown: Wesleyan University Press.'

Smith, Robert G. (1973) *Here's music, a reference book for Fiji schools,* Suva: Ministry of Education, Youth & Sport.

Somerville, Ian Keith (1986) *The Ramayan Mandali movement: popular Hindu theism in Fiji, 1879-1979,* Master's thesis, University of Sydney.

'Tourist' (1937) 'The diary of an English visitor', in Roth 1937: 141-58

Toynbee, Jason and Dueck, Byron (eds) (2912) *Migrating music,* New York: Routledge.

Trnka, Susanna (2008) *State of suffering. Political violence and community survival in Fiji,* Ithaca: Cornell University Press.

Tuqota, Finau Hu'akau (2006) *A critical examination of the music curriculum in Fiji secondary schools with reference to indigenous Fijian music: a study of four schools,* MA thesis, University of the South Pacific.

University of Manchester, Morgan Centre (2009) Turning personal', http://www.socialsciences.manchester.ac.uk/morgancentre/events/2009/turning-personal/.

Usher, Len and Leonard, Hugh (1979) *This is radio Fiji. Twenty-five years of service*

1954-1979, Suva: Fiji Broadcasting Commission.

Williams, Thomas (1870) *Fiji and the Fijians, and missionary labours among the cannibals; extended with notices of recent events; by James Calvert,* ed. George Stringer Rowe, 3rd ed., London: Hodder and Stoughton.

Printed in Great Britain
by Amazon